THE COMING CONVERGENCE
OF WORLD RELIGIONS

THE COMING CONVERGENCE OF WORLD RELIGIONS

ROBLEY EDWARD WHITSON

NEWMAN PRESS
New York/Paramus/Toronto

CONTENTS

For
J. Franklin Ewing
Teacher and Friend

*   *   *

The Master said: As to being a Divine Sage
or even a man of Goodness, far be it from me to
make any such claim. But as for unwearying effort
to learn and unceasing patience in teaching others,
these are merits I do not hesitate to claim.

The studies undertaken here below soar on high,
and perhaps after all I am known by Heaven.

Analects VII: 33 and XIV: 37

PREFACE

Reaching back into the late Nineteenth Century with the development of the comparative study of religion, we can trace the origins of serious interest in the possibility of a unity in the religions of mankind. Although now we can easily recognize the simplistic character of the earlier attempts to formulate a unitive interpretation of religion—centered upon the presumption that all traditions could be reduced to an underlying common core—we must also recognize that the growing contemporary openness in religion could not be taking place without these first explorations.

We are still exploring, of course, but we have now moved across the threshold into a new situation in religion. No longer is the quest for unity primarily the concern of historians, social theorists and those who generally felt themselves to be outside the commitment to one of the traditions. The quest for unity at long last involves those with a specific religious identity and hence enters the very substance of religious experience, both individual and communally shared. Even though a concern still limited to a very few, the explosion in communications and the revolution in

education are even now multiplying the effect of these few astro-
nomically.

The question before us, then, is not whether the world's religious traditions have a positive significance for one another, but
rather, how we can formulate an understanding of that significance. The formulation we seek must arise from within actual
religious experience and be capable of speaking to one who listens from within a tradition of sharing specific historic forms of
experience. It must not presume that the process towards unity
will destroy the various traditions, reducing them to some common, indeterminate kind of religious experience. On the contrary, to be authentic it must recognize and prize the very different heritages, for we can now see that each at its core is
unique. Somehow the differing traditions, originating in isolation
from each other and so coming to their present maturity separately, are to become dimensions of one another, complementing
each other by their varied uniquenesses, and making possible an
undreamed of breadth and depth of vision for man in an infinite
universe.

This study is an exploration of the new situation of religion in
terms of a corresponding new situation of theology. If a formulation of the unitive in religion must come from within actual religious experience, then it calls for a new kind of theological enterprise, one no longer confined within the field of interest of one
tradition only. Theology as a discipline must be opened up to the
full range of meaning which religious experience and its sharing
is becoming.

This exploration began experientially several years ago in attempts to relate Christian experience outward. The moment was
right in that more and more I found others, Christian and non-
Christian, drawn to the same task, and hence I was able to encounter growing sources of influence to shape my own awareness
of this new creative thrust. The concluding chapter of this book,
"Convergence and Commitment," is in many ways a model for
the evolutionary development of all that is attempted here. It

began as a brief response paper contributed to the first Gallahue Conference on World Religions sponsored by Princeton Theological Seminary in 1964. The critical reaction of the conference participants provoked a rethinking and reformulation, much of which came to constitute the concluding chapter of *Mysticism and Ecumenism* published two years later. For the second Gallahue Conference in 1966, I was called upon to prepare a session paper, "The Situation of Theology," which became the core of the present book. (The original paper was published with the other Conference papers in *Religious Pluralism and World Community*, edited by Edward J. Jurji; Leiden: E. J. Brill: 1969.) Reaction to this paper also provoked rethinking and reformulation—and hence this book—which led to further revision of the earlier material, published in 1968 as "Religious Convergence and Commitment" in *The Hartford Quarterly* (vol. viii, no. 4). Further reaction has called for further thinking, and so the present concluding chapter is the fourth stage of what clearly will be a continuing evolution. The developmental experience has led me to the conclusion that it is most unlikely I will ever feel satisfied with any formulation of this content or shape as final. And so the concluding chapter is not a conclusion, but an open end and in an evolutionary process whose history thus far has exhibited the mutations to be expected in any discontinuous continuity.

The preparation of this exploration into religious convergence began with a year as a Visiting Scholar at Princeton Theological Seminary (1967–68), and I wish to make grateful acknowledgment to the Seminary community generally for the year of research and congenial living, and particularly to President James I. McCord and Professors Edward Jurji and Seward Hiltner for their continued interest and encouragement. Among those who participated in the Gallahue Conferences, especially helpful criticisms were offered by Professors Wilfred Cantwell Smith, K. S. Murty, Fazlur Rahman, Wing-Tsit Chan, Hajime Nakamura, K. N. Jayatilleke, Ismail Faruqi, Kenneth W. Morgan, Huston Smith and Robert C. Zaehner.

Three former Fordham colleagues, W. Norris Clark, James Sadowski and Beatrice Bruteau, provided the invaluable service of acting as sounding-boards at various stages of the development of the original Princeton Conference papers.

I am indebted to Gregory Baum for a critical reading of the manuscript and suggestions for clarifications in the introductory chapter, incorporated in the footnote regarding the expansion of Nineteenth and Twentieth Century Christian theological horizons. I am also indebted to Thomas O'Brien, my colleague at The Hartford Seminary Foundation, for reviewing the materials and interpretation drawn from Thomas Aquinas.

In addition to the close friendship and continuing theological collaboration I have enjoyed over the last several years with Professor Ewert Cousins, I wish to express special gratitude to him for leading me into the material of Bonaventure and for his critical review of the chapter on the revelational in religion. His courtesy in allowing the incorporation of a major portion of his article on theological models (the appendix) enriches this book with a dimension of creative scholarship of the greatest importance for the integrality of the interreligious dialogue.

Finally, in dedicating this book to the late J. Franklin Ewing I hope to begin, at least, some repayment of the great debt I happily owe him. Although masters cannot be held responsible for their disciples, they must be credited with the foundation of whatever good the disciples might accomplish. I enjoyed the privilege of doing all my formative study in anthropology under his direction. He was a scientist and humanist and a dedicated priest, a uniquely whole person, of mind and spirit, capable therefore of imparting a singleness of vision to his students—inspiring in us a sense of the unity of man in his universe, and all in the One Sacred. One of the very few colleagues and friends of Teilhard de Chardin during the final years of his spiritual exile, he also taught us by example something of the personal courage demanded in the search for truth.

He forgave my wandering from anthropology to theology when he realized my intention was to attempt to "anthropologize" theology, and I began my academic career as his assistant in the Institute of Mission Studies at Fordham University in 1960. During the next several years as a member of the Fordham theological faculty, our times together were less frequent than they should have been, due to his failing health. But each encounter further enriched me personally and inevitably continued my education. And in a very real way he planted and began the nurture of many seeds of this book.

The man who knows the truth is not the equal of him who loves it, and the one who loves it is not the equal of him who delights in it.

(Analects VI: 18)

Robley Edward Whitson

The United Institute
Bethlehem, Connecticut

INTRODUCTION

I

Revolution is the word beyond all others which marks this century and all its works. It seems that there is no facet of man's life which escapes the sweep of changes so profound and irreversible that even now the world really looks *different*. Though the pace of the revolution is uneven—just now reaching into the daily lives of the masses of Asians and Africans—it accelerates with every advance. The attitudes toward the revolution differ markedly: some are triumphalistic in identifying it narrowly with their particular ideological vision; some are possessive in identifying it with one or another aspect of the cult of progress, as a revolution only in science and technology; some are apprehensive or terrified with the loss of easy security and identity; finally, some are hostile anti-revolutionaries, fighting every possible rear guard action in a tragic attempt to turn time back.

Understandably, there are few who can regard the revolution realistically, accepting it for what it is in the process of man's continuing emergence. We speak easily of evolution and its conti-

1

nuity through discontinuity, but the reality as lived remains a shock. We tend to react to it as totally unexpected, forgetting the century of expectation preceding ours. For the revolution began in that "remote" world, with its roots still older. We can identify the tangible beginnings with the American Revolution and its proclamation: *A New Order of the Ages*. This was not simply a matter of colonies overthrowing the political rule of an imperial power (for its time revolution enough!), it was the practical establishment of a new and universalistic ideology of human society: pluralism—in *people* as the source of all determinations. The revolution thus opened with a bold paradox: the norm for the constitution of human society must rest in man's own experience, and man must be both authentically unified and authentically diverse—one and free.

We tend to forget the impact of this opening of the revolution —especially since all too many of the direct descendants of these early revolutionaries have become anti-revolutionaries. The American Revolutionary War, the first of many during the two succeeding centuries, concluded with the surrender of Lord Cornwallis, whose army marched to the field of the surrender ceremonies while its band played "The World Turned Upside Down." As the rest of the world waited confidently for the collapse of republican democracy, within the decade the revolution had been exported to France and Europe. With all its false starts, reversals and subversions, the revolutionary process has continually advanced to challenge eventually every community and way of life.

It is ironic that we do not always recognize many specific movements within this process as proper component parts of the overall revolution, or, in reverse, that we tend to identify one or another part as *the* revolution. We are involved in a total process affecting the entire human situation, a complex universal revolution composed of a variety of special revolutions: political, social, intellectual and spiritual.

Revolution is the proper context for the understanding of all that is involved in contemporary religion. The call to religion to be or to become *relevant* is the call to participate in revolution, and this at its most significant level. For if truly all of civilization is undergoing a total transformation, breaking through into a new dimension of human self-consciousness, then the relevance of religion must be located in this process. The revolution takes place on many levels—much of it on the surface of things in terms of the proliferation of technology, the manipulation of the shape of the environment, the plotting out of practical means-to-ends. The deeper levels reach into man himself, not just his external doings—a new kind of self-consciousness in which somehow he must be fully himself and simultaneously fully unified with others, a new kind of meaning in his relationship with a universal environment neither isolated to this earth nor any longer an antagonist, a new kind of significance for himself and his universe as he asks for a radically new answer to the question: what is Ultimacy for the mankind now emerging?

In the past we have spoken easily of religion as answering man's questions of Ultimacy, and it has. It is neither simplistic nor facetious to assert that religion is always relevant, that there is no problem of irrelevancy. In whatever condition man finds himself he asks *what he is ultimately,* what overarching relationships are open to him so that he can *be greater.* Man has a drive not simply to achieve something greater (mere increase, mere superiority) but toward *greaterness*—an open-ended breakthrough into whatever the total fulfillment he senses can be—the Ultimate, the Transcendent, the Sacred. Religion as the process of asking-and-answering is not an abstraction floating somewhere in space, but a human process: real people do the asking and answering from within the actual situation of their moments of living. And hence the process as such must always be relevant. The particular questions and answers of other people in other life situations may not be relevant to new people in new situations. But insofar as man is in continuity and the religious process of asking-answering is integral to man, religion here and now is always relevant. It is the attempt to isolate particular answers, taking them out of their proper contexts and imposing them as "timeless" norms, which raises the challenge of irrelevancy.

For some, to identify religion as an ongoing process is to rob it of its essential character. Religion is supposed to be independent of time and change, to stand as the one ground of final security; religion *gives* meaning to change and does not *derive* meaning from change. But the problem here is not first the understanding of what religion is, but what change, time, and man's condition as historic are. It is man who is religious—religion is a category of human experience, *man's relatedness* in the Sacred—and thus how we evaluate the ground of religion depends upon how we evaluate man's constitution. To put it simply: if man is essentially static then religion is also essentially static, but if man is non-static then so also is religion.

At the core of the revolution in our civilization is the affirmation of the processual character of man and his universe. This indeed is "the world turned upside down" since for the first time man realizes he was not just "put here" on the earth but has emerged and is emerging from and with the universe. There is something new under the Sun, and every day. A non-static vision of existence is without precedent, and consequently we *feel* its impact precisely insofar as we do not have past patterns at hand which simply need to be adapted to circumstances altered from but of a kind with those of the past. Our problem is one of continuity and discontinuity in which we must find a way of affirming the meaning of the truly and radically new, and at the same time perceive a continuing process of history. In the past it seemed as if history were like a moving stream in which we were carried along; the time-element in which we moved was outside us—it moved and we merely moved with it. In the last analysis we were independent of this flowing, and what we were could be known apart from it; in fact the true values, the ultimate values, were "timeless." Here rested our system of social and individual security, here were the final foundations of religion. The revolution in our sense of history insists that the *static* is an unreal category and, as a word, is nonsense. As existence is processual, time is not an element "outside," but is an integral dimension of the constitution of each and every thing. We do not float in a history which carries us along and which allows us to dissociate what-I-am from what-I-am-doing. History is our "flowing"; it is what we do: we make time.

As this revolution comes to religion we are faced with an enormous task and one not without grave risk. For we must ask and answer new questions—truly new—and also find the means of continuity in what of necessity must remain a single historic process. In every dimension of the revolution there is danger of loss, even destruction, as we seek to create the new, and this is no less true of religion. Whether we are optimistic or pessimistic of the outcome, we have no choice. There is a new heaven and a new earth: the work of religion is to discover its Sacred significance.

II

If we specify our concern with religion as with the Christian Tradition, there are two principal spheres of relevancy and revolution: the newly emerging civilization and the new relationships called for with other religious Traditions. Of course both these spheres comprise the historic situation for any contemporary religion. But as there is really no such thing as religion in general— it is always *this* or *that* tradition as concretized within actual communities—the concrete shape and significance of these spheres vary according to the differing traditions situated in them. Thus, for example, we may speak of the scientific-technological civilization which has taken form in the West as a descendant of "Western Christian Civilization," or as "secular" or "secularized," or as the beginning point of the "post-Christian Era." All such designations express a specific kind of relationship with the Christian Tradition, a relationship radically different from that, say, with the Buddhist Tradition—what would "post-Buddhist Era" express?—or with the Confucian Tradition—how can "secular" point to a contrast with a totally secular religion? In the sphere of religions, relationships differ significantly when we view "other religions" from the vantage point of any one. Thus, the exclusiveness (apparent, at least) of Christianity or Islam necessitates the construction of relationships with other Traditions of a far different sort than those of inclusivistic Hinduism or Buddhism.

The relevance of Christianity to the new civilization is the most prominent religious and theological issue in the West, both within and without the communities of Christians. During the last dozen or so years it has taken the form of a challenge, and the very word *relevance* is often reduced to little more than a slogan. To what is Christianity challenged to be relevant? Popularly, the answer to this question falls into two categories: one oriented directly to individuals, often very isolated individuals, and the other oriented to the new civilization in which the individuals participate. On close examination there really should be but one category, the orientation to the emerging civilization, since it is this revolution in the total way of life identifiable with the massive breakthroughs of science-technology which is the cause of the crisis for individuals, and hence of their questioning of the relevance of Christianity for their lives. The anguish so many experience is precipitated by the sudden loss of stability and security which has come with the across-the-board impact of change in way of life. The achievement of a sense of "place" and "identity" in society can no longer happen the way it did a mere ten or twenty years ago, and we do not yet grasp the functioning of the new way and its values.[1] And so a lost generation, seeking something to bridge the chasm, must question Christianity seriously: does "it" have relevance in the new order of the ages? Or, more demandingly, does *our participation in the Christian experience* mean anything anymore?

One of the most interesting and more readily overlooked features of historic Christianity is its ability to make radical adaptations to its situation in civilization and achieve unassailable relevance in every era. In fact, a recollection of these adaptations can lead us to be wary of this power to be relevant in that all too often it brings with it a subversion of the very values which constitute Christianity as a religious Tradition.

Although other historic instances of Christian adaptations will be considered later, it would be worthwhile at this point to see something concretely of the ambiguity of adaptations. By the close of the persecution period the early Church had already come to terms with Graeco-Roman Civilization, and had "baptized" the ancient philosophers under the formula, "The truth, whoever speaks it, is from the Holy Spirit." [2] Even such sensitive areas as the modes of worship were approached quite pragmatically. Thus Origen, writing before 250 A.D., notes somewhat casually: ". . . the Greeks use Greek . . . the Romans use Latin . . . and everyone prays and sings God's praises as best he can in his own language" [3]—a far cry from the Catholic and Protestant polemics of the Sixteenth Century, or the emotional division among contemporary Catholics at the passing of Latin! Yet in the century following Origen the Fathers of the Church were exercised over the question of music in worship. Jerome was adamant when it came to the use of musical instruments, exclaiming in an admonition on the upbringing of a child: "Let her be deaf to the sound of the organ, and not even know the pipe, the lyre or the cithara." [4] For Chrysostom the issue is one of practicality: "When God saw that many men were lazy and only with difficulty undertook spiritual reading, He desired to make it easy for them, and added a melody to the words of the Prophet, so that rejoicing in the charm of the music all would sing hymns to Him with gladness." [5] Perhaps the best evidence that the Fathers are dealing with the issue of relevance in these instances is provided by those who oppose the majority. Thus, the abbot Pambo decries the use of music precisely because of what we would describe as its secular character: "Woe upon us, my son, for the time has come when monks shall give up the wholesome food from the Holy Spirit, and seek after words and tunes. What is the repentance or what are the tears which come from hymns? What is the repentance in a monk who, whether in church or in his cell, lifts up his voice like a bull?" [6]

The marked differences between Eastern and Western Church traditions are rooted in the different types of relevance demanded by the Greek and Latin wings of the later Empire. The founding of New Rome at Byzantium signalled the beginning of two histories for the Empire and the Churches. At New Rome the ancient Empire would continue another thousand years, with the ultimate leadership of the Christian *Oekoumene* vested in the Emperor—no longer divine, but as *Isopostolos,* the equal of the Apostles. The Eastern Church as a consequence was characteristically dependent upon and identified with the State. In the West old Rome continued but without an Emperor after the deposition of Romulus Augustulus in 476 A.D., and with the incredible task of molding a new kind of society out of the tribes of the barbarian invaders, ultimately with the creation of a new kind of Emperor. In the centuries of upheaval, the Western Church transformed itself into the foundation of the new society, with bishops and abbots more and more acting in the place of civil magistrates and with the Roman Bishop emerging as the ultimate leader, political as well as spiritual, of the Christendom of the Middle Ages. The centuries of struggle between Pope and Emperor are witness to the difficulties which can be inherent in a thorough-going relevance of Church to Society—at least as relevance is popularly conceived.

Examples could be multiplied almost without limit, illustrating the adaptability characteristic of Christianity. And we need not confine such consideration to Christianity. All forms of religion insofar as they speak to the fundamental questions confronting human communities at any moment are relevant in the basic sense of the term. Every religion has come into existence at a point of crisis in the meaning of a community, and remains in existence as long as it continues to make possible the positive confrontation of succeeding crises. And this, of course, is the very heart of the question of relevance for contemporary Christianity:

does Christianity speak meaningfully to the present crisis in civilization, the emergence of the new civilization? Although the answer to this question will have a relationship to the prior history of Christian relevancy, that history as such will not meet the demands of the present crisis—a form of religion which has been relevant in the past can *become* irrelevant for the present and future, and die.

Paradoxically, to be relevant Christianity need not be able to meet the crisis of the *present* generation, those caught in the transition between the old and new ways of life. It is possible (probable?) that nothing can meet this crisis positively: can people reconcile themselves to being *between* identities, to be wanderers in the desert all their lives knowing what they have left and yet never to be *at home?* All of this is by way of suggesting that the setting for the issue of relevance for any religious tradition in the emergence of the new civilization is in the most revolutionary dimensions of what is taking shape.

A new form is being given to all of human life. With the escalation of scientific and technological development the relationship of man to his environment and to himself has changed completely. There is no longer a sense of struggle *against* the world as it is found in its "natural" state. Gone is the old sense of a delicate and at times a precarious balance between what man had succeeded in wresting from Nature and the sudden, unpredictable reassertions of Nature's power over man. In a word, man now is in *control* of his environment, so much so that he is becoming aware of the need to preserve some of it in its wild state! And his relationship to himself has changed just as radically—the same new patterns of knowledge are turned upon his self-knowledge so that a new kind of self-awareness is emerging. With this is joined the prospect of liberation offered by technology, a liberation from the economic necessity of the depression of the mass of men and the consequent positive liberation for life patterns as yet but vaguely defined.

The new civilization is one of paradoxes, of which the most important is probably its drive toward unity coupled with its constantly expanding diversification. All that goes to make science-technology possible demands a high coordination of people and resources, and it also demands increasing specialization among people as the varieties of knowing and doing become ever more complex. For the individual a frustrating tension is formed: he specializes more and more and thereby should be more and more secure in his individuality, but with the numbers of specializations and individuals specializing he tends to feel smaller and smaller, fading into personal insignificance. This aspect of the crisis of identity reflects a more basic issue: what is the relation of individual and society? With the fundamental changes in the cultural context of this question, the older answers no longer apply, and a new answer must be found.

Clearly this is one of the primary entry points of religion into the new civilization insofar as religious traditions are always necessarily concerned with the meaning of man not simply as an isolate individual but as community as well. Liberated mankind, truly capable of being *at home* in his universe, creating new orders of life with new forms of knowledge, seeking a true sense of unity in an expanding diversity, needing a new way to identify himself singly and together—all of this is the fundamental stuff with which contemporary religion must come to grips.

We shall be exploring the issue of unity and diversity for religion within the general context of these dimensions of civilization, but addressing ourselves primarily to the issue of the unity and diversity of the religions themselves. We assume as a basic thesis that for the religious traditions to be relevant for the future they must succeed in manifesting in their own sphere the unitive character of the entire way of life. This means at least two things. First, religious traditions must be capable of speaking positively the language of the new forms of knowing—in place of the grudging and self-defensive concessions and accommodations made to science-technology in the past, which have so alienated religion from the way man really is now. And second, religious traditions must be capable of communication among themselves, discovering the way to unity possible now for the first time in history.

III

From the vantage point of contemporary Christian theology, concern for the thrust toward unity in religion occupies a first place. Unfortunately it does not usually seem to go beyond a concern, and even when it does it is almost always centered upon inter-Christian relationships. By and large, churchmen and theologians have been drawn into a pattern of attempting to construct an inter-Christian unity through resolutions of past historic difficulties (often no longer pertinent), or the utilization of new common grounds (especially as based upon contemporary biblical studies), or the development of common social, economic and political programs, or the like. Whatever short-term and useful advantages might well come from this type of attempt, it is not an approach to unity which arises from the very basis of what constitutes any religious tradition: sharing religious experience. A theology of unity to be valid must address itself to what really happens in a religious community which is taking form precisely in that its members are beginning to sense and share a common life experience somehow in continuity with what can be identified as the Christian Tradition. Inquiries into old credal formulations, new scriptural insights, programs for common action, and the like, are appropriate parts of a theology of unity, but only parts, and only insofar as they are reflective of the growing sharing of religious experience.

A test of theological perception into the issue of unity can be made of Christian theologians by examining the manner in which they approach the relationship of Christianity with other religious Traditions. A certain benignity is usually present, but it is very difficult to find much more. With the rarest of exceptions theologians do not seem ill at ease with their lack of knowledge of

non-Christian Traditions. They are content to draw items here
and there from historians of religion, or to take account of all
other Traditions with a few generalities. It is not an oversimplification to say that Christians simply do not take other Traditions seriously.[7]

Former Secretary General Visser't Hooft of the World Council
of Churches takes a stand congenial to most theologians when he
declares:

The attitude of the Christian Church to the religions can therefore only be the attitude of the witness who points to the one
Lord Jesus Christ as Lord of all men. . . . The Christian Church
cannot therefore participate in the search for a synthesis or confluence of the existing religions. . . . And it would mean that the
Christian Church had given up its identity and integrity.[8]

One can agree that the Christian Church must bear witness to
the historic and existential uniqueness of Christ for all men—otherwise it would not be the Christian Church—yet why must this
preclude a confluence of religious traditions or demand that
Christians abandon their identity? Evidently for Visser't Hooft
and most of those he intends to address, a potential unity carries
the sense of destruction. Even more important, he must be presuming there is nothing in non-Christianity of ultimate significance for all mankind.

Yet he goes on immediately to the possibility of dialogue between Christians and non-Christians:

. . . . I turn to him with the willingness to listen to him, to understand him, to seek mutual enrichment. . . . As a Christian I
cannot do this without reporting to him what I have come to
know about Jesus Christ. . . . I shall be glad to listen to my part-
ner and may learn much from his account of his spiritual journey. . . . It should be done in an attitude which Hocking has so
well defined as "reverence for reverence." The fact that Christians believe they know the source of divine truth does not mean
that they have nothing to learn from men of other faiths.[9]

In view of what he has previously said and implied, is such a dialogue genuine? He does not seem to expect to learn anything of *divine truth*, but simply something of his spiritual journey. "Reverence for reverence" is a noble sentiment, but how does it escape being patronizing? (In a quite different context President Eisenhower once expressed the "other end" of the subjectivism implied in this type of reverence: "Our government makes no sense unless it is founded in a deeply felt religious faith—and I don't care what it is." [10]) And, as we see Visser't Hooft's conception of the future of missionary activity, there appears to be virtually no change in real evaluations of the "heathen," simply a change in technique necessitated by the collapse of colonialism; the fact that "other faiths" feel the call to mission is accounted for both pragmatically in recognizing that they can use the same techniques and triumphalistically in the implication of objective Christian spiritual superiority already established:

[Missionary activity] on the part of the religions must not be the recourse to any form of legal, political or social pressure, but only the spiritual answer of their witness. The coming great encounter of the religions must be a purely spiritual encounter. [11]

He indicates the type of "coming great encounter" among religions as systems mutually closed to one another:

[Cooperation] is undertaken to achieve specific common purposes and not to render common witness to common religious convictions. [12]

[And because we have no common definition of religion] such cooperation must not draw an artificial line of demarcation between those who call themselves religious and those who do not. [13]

This hope for peaceful coexistence among religions comes in terms which clearly have nothing to do with religion as such. *Any organizations*, religious or not, might well enter into cooperation that does not involve anything common to religions. One wonders how the author conceived of these as expressions of specifically religious coexistence—apart from the rejection of the outright hostility which prevailed heretofore.

Among Catholic theologians one who has become a symbol of the creative transition away from a closed to an open theology, Karl Rahner, has been concerned with non-Christian Traditions especially as he looks forward to a near future in which Christianity will have to have a new vision of its role, or at least of the manner in which it plays its role, in continuing history. Rahner's concern for the other Traditions, thus, is from within a specifically Christian context of problems: Christians as a minority of humanity (at least for as long as we can now foresee), Christians living in a secular world, Christians giving witness in a post-Christian Era.

He leads us into the problem to be faced by his Christian of the future in a far from positive manner:

. . . . Everywhere the non-Christian and the anti-Christian will have full and equal rights and may perhaps by threat and pressure contribute to give society its character and may perhaps even coalesce in powers and principalities as forerunners and manifestations of Anti-Christ.[14]

Far from seeing any creative possibilities for Christianity in the new civilization, Rahner projects a Christianity in a religious ghetto almost completely alienated from the rest (the overwhelming majority) of mankind:

The Christians will be the little flock of the Gospel, perhaps esteemed, perhaps persecuted, perhaps bearing witness to the holy message of their Lord with clear and respected voice in the polyphonic or cacophonous chorus of ideological pluralism, perhaps only as an undertone, from heart to heart.[15]

Rahner rejects fully any underlying principle of unity in man's religious experience (excepting insofar as it ultimately gives way to Christianity):

That future Christian will be living as a member of the little flock in an immeasurably vast world of non-Christians. How in such circumstances is he to think of his Church? How is he to live with the Church's inalienable consciousness that it is founded by God, by Christ the Lord of all history, that it is the sole eternally valid religion? [16]

. . . . The Church is not the society of those who alone are saved, but the sign of the salvation of those who, as far as its historical and social structure are concerned, do not belong to it. . . . What is there expressed may fall on deaf ears and obdurate heart in the individual and may bring judgment instead of salvation.[17]

The theological consolation of the future Christian is pure and unadulterated triumphalism, perhaps a psychological necessity for one caught in a ghetto:

This Christian of the future . . . knows that the morning light on the mountains is the beginning of the day in the valley, not the light of day above condemning the darkness beneath. The Christian will, therefore, go out into the world serenely, without anguish.[18]

Visser't Hooft and Rahner have both developed positions from which they hope for a dialogue with the "rest of mankind," especially in terms of religions and ideologies. Unfortunately, undertaking religious dialogue under the conditions stated would simply be dishonest. The "reverence for reverence" which Visser't Hooft feels effectively cuts off reverence from experience in any but the most subjectivistic sense. For them dialogue cannot be entered into on the questions of ultimate value—but these are precisely the questions of religion. Ironically, they imply the subversion of proper religious concerns by encouraging the substitution of pragmatic concerns (which, in all probability, can be better handled by philosophers, poets and social scientists than by religionists as such).[19]

One gets the strong impression that the apparent retreat from religious imperialism on the part of the future Christian is not the result of a principle but simply the frustration of "sour grapes." Is there anything in the theological formulations that precludes a reunion of sword and cross in the future when Rahner's sunlight on the mountains once again dispels the darkness below?

One of the most interesting problems not faced for the future Christian may be posed as a question: can there be any ghetto in the future? The ghetto, for any purpose, is possible only if isolation in way of life is possible. Will such be the situation of the new civilization? Even the most superficial consideration of the effects of mass communications leads one to doubt if people can be long kept in isolation from the experiences of others. As the most profound of those experiences reach into the heart of any religious tradition, can the Christian of the future remain unaware of the impact of the non-Christian Traditions?

This is the immediate context of our exploration of the convergence of religions, and it is truly revolutionary if we take the constituting factors seriously. Final evaluations will rest on the choice we make of our initial presumption: are systems of religion *closed* or *open* to each other? Put very simply, we will be exploring what emerges if we hold that religious traditions are open to each other. This will require us to speak to two principal needs: how to give meaning to the relationship of the new religious situation with the new civilization, and how to find ways to articulate the creative relationships among religions. Our real task, therefore, is to explore what would constitute a theology or theologies for religious convergence. If religious traditions are the sharing of religious experience, we must develop systems of language which will allow us to express the new kind of sharing beginning to take place—the many which *somehow* are dimensions of each other in a greater unity not destructive of its constituting communities.

THE
UNITY
OF
CIVILIZATION

I

The unity of mankind, although still in large part a dream, is beginning more and more to evoke a sense of reality. Both the dream and the reality express the unique character of the Twentieth Century.

Without parallel in the past, contemporary civilization is coming to be centered upon the consciousness of man as community: the significance of man in personal relationship—not the isolated individual nor the subordinating society. Yet, paradoxically, the historic situation of contemporary civilization bears sad witness to both human isolation and subordination. Perhaps this is the most impressive element in the development of the first half of the century: materialist individualism, exalting the pragmatic good in the isolated value of possession, pleasure, security—the individual opposed to others, morally unrelated; and subordinating totalitarianism, identifying all reality in the will of one as leader, as consensus, as collective dictatorship—the individual absorbed in anti-relational conformism.

17

In the latter half of the century we find that our choice does not rest between these two. It seems, rather, that opposition to both is stimulating an awareness of a positive correspondence between man as individual and as social: community. And an immediate consequent of even the most rudimentary recognition of human community is the further recognition of human unity, not simply in terms of external pressures and circumstances pragmatically forcing man to come together, but as an emerging consciousness of what man really is, and hence the consciousness that these "external" factors are not determinative causes, but dynamic reflections of the human condition.

Yet human unity has not attained more than a *sense* of reality for us. It is still clearly at its beginnings, still mostly dream. But perhaps now we can see it as a dream in the psychological sense —a sign from within the hidden inward side of our process of consciousness revealing our fuller life history—rather than a dream in the sense of theoretical ideal. The thrust toward unity in contemporary civilization is unique precisely because it has emerged in our consciousness from our real, experiential history, not from an abstract social theory. We can see this best in terms of problems. The sense of reality we have about human unity does not rest upon what has been achieved, but upon the appalling problems experienced (and only partly resolved) in the first half of the century and upon the problems now arising as we seek unity.

While stressing the uniqueness of our present situation and thus implying truly new issues calling for truly new modes of confrontation, unity as a dream reflecting the inner process of human history requires us to seek to understand that history as a continuity. The uniqueness of the present cannot be an unrelated or discontinuous uniqueness, unless we would be willing to proclaim the discovery of an absolutely new human species and history, not evolved, not a process, but some sort of spontaneous creation *ex nihilo.* The uniqueness of the present is to be located in the emergence into our consciousness of the drive toward a real and realizable unity, a consciousness of present experience pointed into the future but grown from the past with all its non-conscious implications.

Placed in such a context, the dream of unity has a very real history and reflects truly the process of existence. Whatever we observe in our world—the greatest thing, the smallest—we discover the same problem of meaning: how is it itself, and how is it that it does not exist by itself? This question must be asked when we look into the inner constitution of things, observing the variety of elements and yet the greater identity achieved somehow together. This holds true, even more impressively, when we consider things in terms of their process of existence rather than as if they exist statically as at a moment isolated from other moments. While they are real at each instant, their significance is known only insofar as we see what they *do,* what *happens* among them, the *effect* they have on one another—that they are not static, but "flow."

The inner meaning of the dream of unity becomes more evident when we consider living reality. Our most secure understanding of the basis of living things rests upon the recognition of their degree of organization. In a manner of speaking, the living are more unified, quantitatively and qualitatively, than "other" things. Their constituting elements are less able to preserve their identity apart from each other, and the effect of the unity of elements is dramatically beyond the individual elements themselves. Yet the reality of the living whole depends upon the *unity* of the *individuals,* both factors, and it is not possible to theorize a supposed ultimacy or priority for one or the other. In fact, the observation of assimilation of new elements and procreation of new wholes insists that we approach our understanding in terms of coordination.

When we think of human history we tend to see the great diversity in mankind: the long evolutionary sequence with its many kinds of men; the widely scattered peoples and tribes with all their differing ways of life; the separate races, languages and traditions embodied in more recent millennia in great cities and civilizations. Yet, if we look closely we see this vast diversity in human expression in a process of convergence: slowly and at times in almost chaotic disorder more and more interrelation takes place—separate kinds of men become fewer, hardly any men are now scattered out of contact with each other, the races move together, common languages are sought and heretofore isolate traditions are cross-fertilizing one another, and all set in new cities and civilizations becoming so vast and hence moving so close to one another that the boundaries are becoming lost. And now we can see man's world from beyond it in space, and that world is clearly *round* with all parts leading to all others.[1]

It is *one whole world,* but man is not now whole, not yet significantly one. And the interpretation of the process of existence and history as convergent does not guarantee man's ultimate unity. Man can fail. We have lived with the terror of that possibility for a full generation. For the first time we actually have in our hands the tools to forge our unity or our self-destruction. To know that the dream of unity is a reflection of what we really are and are to be does not mean that the dream must come true. The reality which the dream symbolizes can be suppressed, kept from consciousness and fulfillment by our suicide.

Putting aside any attempt to estimate the chances of survival, highly subjective at best, is the direction of human development actually toward unity, and if so toward what kind of unity? The evaluation of the ultimate effect of man's present direction of development is not self-evident. The same data can be interpreted in quite opposite ways. Yet there is an interesting point of departure all would seem to agree upon with little hesitation: the data show us *man is evolving,* either toward a greater unity or toward a more and more irreconcilable state of division. (Hardly anyone seems to think man is not evolving in any direction!) The opposition of the two evaluations is certainly reflective of a prior optimism or pessimism—which sooner or later leads again to the question of future survival since both would agree that man's dividedness contains within it the threat of self-destruction, a threat increasing or decreasing proportionately with the actual presence or absence of the elements of division.

In one very real sense the interpretation of our development as unitive (or divisive) is not simply an objective judgment, it is an option. The data of human experience are not "outside" the historic process, and the process in its human dimension is directly *what men do* within the range of possibilities open at any one point in the full context of the historic situation. The observer is also, and primarily, a participant, a doer. Thus the real meaning of the question of our possible unity is: *will we do it?* But as the option is not absolute, being contained within the boundaries set both by non-human factors and the cumulative effect of all previous options, the answer will not be found except in the context in which the option can be made: the range of possibilities as these possibilities actually exist at the moment of choosing and hence as they limit, condition and motivate the choosing.

II

If we follow a positive interpretation the questions of the development toward increasing unity and of the type of unity being formed become a single question embodying our understanding of the context through which the development is taking place. We have already characterized the unitive process as convergent, and it is this notion which will be used as the norm of the present attempted analysis. In an evolving process in which a variety of heretofore separate factors come to be formed into a new whole— a qualitatively and organizationally new entity beyond the additive effect of the no longer separate component elements—the new whole is not something discontinuous from the previous moment of the process. Though it may be radically different from any of the entities of that previous moment, it is continuous *with the process* in that it takes origin through the interrelation that occurs at one moment among elements previously unrelated in this manner. Our most forceful specification of convergence in process is probably that of biological generation, in which the offspring is clearly a new reality not identifiable singly with the parents. It is not simply an addition of their characteristics, but something quite different; yet in origin of individual existence it is in complete continuity with them: it embodies them in the greater effect of their convergence.

Conditioned by the primitive mechanical vision of existence of pre-contemporary science and philosophy, we tend to see ourselves and our universe as an accumulation of separate entities, basically static in themselves but moving deterministically in relation to one another only because each has been "set going." Everything will eventually "run down" and the haphazard relations of one to the other will again be resolved and cease. In terms of human history we tend to see separate individuals, gathered only conveniently into groups, and acting *upon* one another in a long series of essentially external cause and effect relationships. There is nothing but a linear succession of *this* producing *that,* and *that* replacing *this.* In such a mechanistic vision of the process of development if unity were to be produced it would be a "new thing" which would replace the previous situation of non-unity, and such replacement would be necessarily destructive of what had gone before. It is important here to see the effect of linking the two questions: *will there be unity?* and *what type will it be?* A mechanistic unity inevitably is a *uniformity:* many individual elements are *made into* something not diverse, and hence not a *unity of things* but *one new thing* made out of its predecessors in such a way that it displaces them—they are in themselves destroyed. A mechanistic unity is actually no unity at all, but is simply the elimination of diversity. A *new thing* now exists, and the "old things" have been absorbed into it, reduced from what they were in themselves to being mere parts in the machine, without their own authenticity, and subject to replacement if it suits the well-being of the machine.

Translated into the sphere of human relationships, this vision is the basis of the horrors of nearly four centuries: the political and religious absolutism of crown and later nationalistic state, economic absolutism of the industrial revolution, the totalitarian ideologies. Each claims to produce unity, but actually produces a "new thing" conformity, in which the individual human as such is a mere part. In man's sacred relationships this vision has produced religious and ideological imperialism, in which the experience of Absolute has been twisted into an absolute experience calling for destruction of sacred relationships which have made the present moment possible but which do not *conform*.

Is this kind of unity unity at all? Not if unity means somehow bringing the diverse into significant interrelationship without destroying them—the opposite to uniformity. Mechanistic unity must be something external, determined from without and not reflective of any supposed inward thrust of things themselves. It is not convergence but conformity. Can such a "unity" be achieved? We are in the midst of that issue, still unresolved. Our century stands in sad witness to the emergence of effective social totalitarianism with its ideological imperialism. And three paths are still open to us: conformism, separate coexistence or convergence.

Perhaps it is significant that when we attempt to articulate a world view liberated from and opposed to the mechanistic we can describe it only negatively as non-mechanistic. We have not yet succeeded in settling upon a designation which would positively and adequately identify what we are catching sight of as we move away from the closed vision of the machine. We should be reminded by this of the newness of the vision, the still primitive condition of our experience of openness and the fact that for most of mankind it is only the practical effects of the new vision which have been experienced, not the vision itself. As a consequence we have not yet been able to develop a non-mechanistic language and hence it is very difficult to communicate the new experience—which for the most part must be achieved directly in one way or another, rather than be initiated through communicational sharing. The child is still drawn into Western society with a conditioning into a vision of things as separate elements in basically external relationships. He sees his parents acting first and foremost as individuals who *concede* areas of life and action to others in society. He learns to speak of "them": society, government, church, fellow citizens, the human race.

The difficulty in correlating in life the old vision of things with the already felt implications of the new (especially where there is no conscious suspicion that there is a new vision) can be seen in the contradictory symptoms of the total tension of the contemporary situation. Thus, coupled with widespread revolt against the patterns of conformity is the deep need very forcefully expressed for group acceptance (and a powerful social sanction of excommunication for all who fail to conform to the revolt). With great devotion to causes of idealism there is the all too common failure to focus commitment upon actual human beings, preferring, for example, the liberation of "peoples" and "races," and outright rejection of "classes" and "generations."

For those caught in the transition from the mechanistic to the non-mechanistic, the goal of the developmental process is not seen as unity but as coexistence. Individuality is strongly asserted and minimal social interrelation is conceded, with a positive confidence in direct personal experience as the means of resolving the tension. This is still a mechanistic vision—the elements are essentially individual and not internally constituted in interrelationship, but only passing into (and out of) relationships according to external circumstances. It is the mechanistic which is adapted to the already experienced practical consequences of the non-mechanistic, through the emphasis on direct experience. And this both fulfills the beginnings of the truly contemporary situation and also thwarts it.

Direct experience demands that we see things from the "inside," that we not be content with description or external effects. It calls upon us to take seriously the present moment, what we are and what we are doing, and to extend this seriousness to all— persons and things—who are together with us in this moment. It does not allow us to prefer the security of retreat to the risk of involvement. Ironically, at the same time the emphasis on direct experience can make it impossible for us to enter the reality of the contemporary situation, if direct experience is approached through the unconscious acceptance of the mechanistic vision of the universe. For in that case our experience is divisive: the present moment and its importance are seen as standing against others, past and future, since all are discontinuous; all value must be concentrated exclusively in the present experience, with other dimensions of experience—our own or others'—denied as value-charged, lest a comparison of differing values undercut our commitment to the narrowed present. Fundamentally, mechanistically formed direct experience must so emphasize the individual experiencer that significant communication of experience from one to another becomes impossible, even though, tragically, this is the very thing sought!

Hence, the further significance of the diversity of people and things cannot be seen in terms of unity, for in the response to direct personal experience where the authenticity of both person and experience cannot be maintained except by evading integral relationships any unity must mean uniformity. In a mechanistic world coexistence must be the optimistic option.

III

There is a profound difference between the older classic mechanistic vision and the contemporary emphasis on experience. The quest for the experiential marks the decisive movement away from the mechanistic, although as long as it remains a negative response—moving away from—the tension of the transition cannot be resolved, nor can a unitive pattern be envisioned genuinely alien to a conformity. A positive response in which the transition can move to completion will involve the achievement of personal experience but beyond the context of the *individual basically alone*—the mechanistic heritage—and thus neither conformity nor coexistence will be within the range of possibilities open to the fulfillment of the historic process. A non-mechanistic world excludes the static, the isolate and the closed, insisting on a dynamic process of existence open to all that can happen from "inside." And thus the absolutizing of neither the *one* nor the *many* is possible.

The experience of individuation involves both the assertion of the authenticity of each element in itself and the assertion that no element exists simply in itself but in essential interrelation with others, ultimately each interrelated to all others. The interrelation is essential, deriving its significance from the constitution of the individual, from "within." Since individuals are constantly in change both in themselves and in their relationships, their interrelatedness is necessarily dynamic, and this dynamism is also essential, from "within." Fundamentally, the experience of reality evaluated in a non-mechanistic framework is that of process: the vast multitude of individuals, wholly themselves and totally interrelated in a dynamic unity of many—many individuals and many relationships. From one vantage point the process is singular, the ultimate unity of all things; from another the process is unimaginably complex, involving all the processes of every possible individual and group in all their relationships. Whatever the level of our observation, this is our *experience* of reality, not one *or* many, but one *and* many, a basic paradox in which the authenticity of every individual as such must be maintained and yet never as if unrelated.

Within a processual understanding of reality, any unity must be seen as one of convergence: unity formed out of actual individuals which somehow do not cease to be themselves within the unity. Convergence excludes the isolation of individuals—there simply are none existing alone; convergence also excludes a unity in the sense of uniformity—any interrelation must be an interrelation of individuals or groups of individuals.

When we translate this in terms of man's way of life it is quite clear that we are witnessing the formation of dramatic new relationships arising from and involving many kinds of ways of life heretofore basically separate in both their development and their effects. We speak of the emergence of a world civilization but if this is within the context of convergence such a civilization will have to be both singular—a way of life for a unified mankind—and plural—derived from the world of many traditions and meaningful for a world of many kinds of individuals. A realistic world civilization must be fundamentally pluralistic; for men, real historic men, have been formed in great diversity and have achieved genuinely fulfilling values in ways simply not the same. Nor are the values in their entirety the same, but have an all important internal variety which can be grasped the moment we cease thinking of human value as an abstraction and begin recognizing it as it is actually lived out integrally within a way of life.

The emergence of a singularity in civilization, dependent upon the development of radically new elements in human life and hence of new relationships whereby they can be shared, strangely enough makes more significant all that has developed separately. Brought together through the new relationships of sharing, the now mutually available varieties create a complex of choices for men, and different needs can be filled from a more open range of possibilities. In convergence, the singularity in civilization rests upon the degree of sharing open to the participants in which common achievement is made possible, especially the achievement of the communication of experience. Many come to share experience in important and broad areas of life. Yet this singularity in no way excludes a true variety. The two are brought into a dynamic relationship. Individuals who are not the same come to share experience together, and from this come to understand the basis of their individuality and finally to see that *valuable* differences are complementary rather than divisive. Convergence, then, presumes that the unresolved and unresolvable paradox of the one and the many is the positive key to the understanding of what is taking place in man's way of life: unitive pluralism—men are becoming truly one insofar as *all* that they are can be brought into dynamic interrelationship.

Regardless of the logic in the attempt to analyze the basic pattern of a unitive pluralism, one way or another we must always return to the practical question: *is convergence taking place?* This is not to ask: *will unitive pluralism actually be the pattern of the future?* We are not required to predict a future fulfillment of the present direction of development, but to assess that direction as it now appears. At this stage we need not become involved in the optimistic or pessimistic options discussed earlier. With regard to its final result (dependent upon countless factors still unrecognized or still to come to bear) we recognize the hazard of predicting, yet we can inquire into the type of pattern now evolving in terms of objectively observed factors now present which must be accounted for and which certainly will form at least part of our future.

Without doubt the most important single factor in contemporary development is that of communication, in the most extensive sense of all that makes possible and/or inevitable the sharing of experience. The fundamental issue in the unitive side of convergence is the degree in which experience is shared—not simply newly forming areas of experience but experience already formed in the past separateness of the pluralist variety, the other side of convergence.

We recognize in the sharing of experience, whatever the scale, another basic paradox which must be dealt with if we are to approach any human situation realistically. Experience as such takes place within individual consciousness and partakes of the uniqueness of the individual. Yet experience always has the possibility of extending beyond the individual because whatever the object of experience might be it is independent of the subject, and because among individuals the biological-psychological means of experiencing are common. Since each individual is a distinct entity in terms of "equipment" and since there can be no exact reduplication of the total formative process whereby each is *exactly himself* at the moment of any experience, what occurs must be genuinely unique to the individual. And yet at the same time something proper to the experience can be communicated to others (at least communication is attempted) so that they can share the original experience by the evocation of a related experience in themselves. (Perhaps the paradoxical character of the situation becomes most evident in those instances in which communication of the most intimate experience is attempted, where, in effect, the individual seeks to make available to another that which is directly reflective of his self-identification, his uniqueness.)

The success of the communication of experience is the basis of human culture, civilization and tradition. What is learned in immediate experience by one individual can enter the experience of another by communication rather than by an independent reduplication of the experience. There thus takes place a cumulative effect of experience in which one level is "inherited" through communication rather than rediscovered. And hence the starting point of the new level of experience is the end point of the previous, which alone makes possible the development of complex ways of life—civilizations.

There is something more to this sharing of experience, however, another dimension beyond what might be thought of as a horizontal and vertical system of transferal. The experience of sharing experience (either by one communicating his individual experience to another, or by the cumulative communication of one level of development as the basis for another) shapes our way of experiencing, so that in the very process as it takes place within the individual consciousness our experience tends to be formed in a manner easily allowing for or even demanding communication. All of our conscious reflections of experience are psychologically conscious through symbols, mostly language symbols. These are themselves the devices of communication, the commonly developed indicators derived from previous attempts at sharing. Thus, something significant in all of our conscious thought is, in a manner of speaking, already "packaged" for transfer to another. And we observe that in normal circumstances we find ourselves not merely capable of communication but urged to it. A value is seen in having others share in our own experience. Further, there is a special value in sharing experience as a community by placing ourselves in situations where we each experience some common factor simultaneously and then bring our communicable evaluation together immediately into a common pattern.

Quite obviously, a radical extension of these dimensions of communication increases proportionately any process toward unity. The more that is shared experientially, and the more effectively this is extended (both in terms of the numbers of people involved and the degree of intensity of the involvement), the greater will be the development of singularity in the pattern of interrelationships. As the Twentieth Century progresses isolated individuals and societies are becoming less and less possible. We have already moved rapidly from a welter of closed human systems to a few—with the drive toward openness as yet unresolved but a principal element in the evolving pattern. There is one certainty at present: the radical extension of the dimensions of communication is continuing in so extraordinary a fashion that only an unknown intervening factor of the future could make possible the continuance of past human isolation.

IV

But communication by itself cannot be the basis of a convergent unity. Effective extension of the sharing of experience could issue in a rigid uniformity, a possibility rightly feared at present. The elimination of a number of closed systems could result in the emergence or survival of a single closed system (at least for as long as a non-processual world view could be maintained). Convergence requires both the movement of a variety toward significant unity, and also significant variety within that unity. "Significant" in both instances, while not allowing for actual definition except insofar as the unfolding process of development actually takes place, indicates the recognition of the need for actual interrelationship of real individuals. Unity to be significant must embrace relationships allowing individuals to experience a true common identity in complement to their self-identity. Variety to be significant must provide real options in the range of human possibilities and insure that the unitive shape of life will remain open to all that it can be in a future development.

Correlated with communication in the contemporary pattern of civilization is its complementing factor of specialization. The cumulative effect of our shared experience has been the opening of more and more specialized areas of experience, each requiring its own mode of approach and further extension. We have but to observe the progressive development of the empirical sciences over the last century to realize the openness which specialization demands. Each specialization becomes a *way to reality* differing from other ways and not reducible to them. Yet at the same time these proliferating developments more and more demand effective intercommunication so that specializations will not become isolated and meaningless to the rest of life experience, but will come into unity and thus be meaningful. Extend this basic pattern of scientific concern to the other areas of our civilization and it is evident that insofar as specialization—scientific, technological, artistic, economic, political—is a rising factor, diversity becomes proportionately characteristic of the development toward unity.

Reflecting all that contributes to the possibility of a world civilization, unified and diverse, and speaking from the vantage point of contemporary Asia, K. M. Panikkar draws our attention to two sides of convergence:

Any return to a purely Asian tradition is ruled out by the growth of social, economic and political forces which no country in Asia had to deal with in the past. . . . Though the influence of Europe and the penetration of new ideas have introduced vast changes in Asia, and may lead to even greater changes, Asian civilizations will continue to develop their marked individuality and remain spiritually and intellectually separate from Christian Europe.[2]

Although still in general terms, we have here the recognition of the concrete process of convergence as it is occurring in the experience of heretofore separate sections of mankind. The continuance of "a purely Asian tradition" is no longer possible, but, implicitly, neither is that of a purely European tradition. The social, economic and political forces previously unknown in Asia are not simply being imported into Asia from Europe, but are operative in both spheres of civilization, more and more becoming the factors of integrating shared experience and hence more and more becoming formative agents for a unified way of life.

However, this unity is seen as convergent, embracing profound differences with every prospect that the Asian civilizations will develop in ways reflecting those differences. Perhaps our best example of what this can mean is to be found in contemporary Japan, the complex outgrowth of a century of the deep interpenetration of two quite different kinds of civilization. Both the extraordinary interchanges and the violent antagonisms of this remarkable history point to the dynamic tensions set in motion by the convergent process. Although it is still far too early to attempt any long-term prediction concerning the final shape of Japanese life, it is evident that the Japanese have not simply been "Westernized," nor have they segregated Western and older Japanese dimensions of their civilization into controlled departments. Even though the interfunctioning of the two forces is now at a relatively rudimentary level of integration, it is clear that all aspects of Japanese life are involved in both. Japan is not "Westernized," it has not been merely made over into a Western-style country, and Japan cannot ever return to its pre-Western history.

For Japan and all centers of difference in culture (including Europe and America) the question of evaluating the process of convergence is not so much the concern with the factors here and now tending toward the unification of experience as with those which now and in the future will be the foundation of the pluralism in that experience. Panikkar formulates this for Asia as a spiritual and intellectual separation from Christian Europe. As a contrast to the increasingly unitive experience in scientific, tech-

nological, social, economic and political spheres, separation according to spiritual and intellectual spheres can be a useful formula to state the paradoxical balance in unitive pluralism, at
least for this moment in history. But on the positive side, what
can the Asian and Western spiritual and intellectual traditions
mean or come to mean to one another? This is an inevitable
question since those who are drawing ever closer in the sharing of
experience cannot be expected for long to segregate arbitrarily
areas of experience which they must always regard as the most
significant of all.

Although we must raise the question and come to such conclusions as we are able concerning its implications for the future of
convergence, we must be aware of the very severe limitations we
work under in any attempt to analyze the present state of the
meeting of East and West in these dimensions. In *World Cultures
and World Religions,* Hendrick Kraemer provides us with a sober
evaluation:

The contemporary encounter or meeting of Orient and Occident
in cultural and religious respect, truly impressive and fascinating
as it may be in many senses, is fundamentally speaking still a superficial matter.[3]

The superficiality of the encounter in this area, in contrast to
that in which our civilizations have begun the process of interpenetration, is due to the fact that the encounter is not taking
place from the "inside," that is, experience in intellectual culture
and religion is not being communicated and shared. With rare
exceptions contact in these spheres is external, involving at most
the syncretistic borrowing of one or another item without recognition of its significance within the full context of meanings in
which it is integrated. Generally speaking, especially in the
sphere of religion very few are struck with the fact that the alien
way they are observing is actually effective, evokes real experience, forms people positively and hence must be taken seriously
as something which has objective significance for men.

But what if the encounter in religion ceases to be superficial? What if the continuing development of the convergent process begins to challenge the spiritual and intellectual separation of peoples?

CONVERGENCE OF RELIGIONS

I

The positive confrontation of religious traditions, or even its possibility, is a recent historical phenomenon. The Spanish discovery of the civilizations of the Americas came as an unexpected shock and, in retrospect, can be recognized as the first in a series of traumatic events which have revolutionized our entire body of intellectual and religious presuppositions. The Sixteenth Century European was not prepared for an entirely new world of peoples and ways of life unaccounted for in the single land mass of Eurasia. Christian-Muslim contact during the Middle Ages involved little or no positive religious interchange since each had theological interpretations of the other which effectively nullified exploratory interest (infidel, demon-worshipper, false prophet, tritheist and so on). For the European the religion of the further East was either idolatry-demonolatry or half-mythical Christian Churches (the Nestorians of China, and the fabulous Prester John). In forcing their flat world into a sphere, the first discoverers quite naturally failed to reckon with an entirely new land mass in the seas

35

between Europe and Asia, and so the new world was the *Indies* where one could expect to find both devil worshippers and the wise Prester John.

The Spanish recognition of the independence of the civilizations of Central and South America called for a new understanding of their religious traditions (ultimately a corresponding new understanding of those of Asia as well). The chronicles of such early Spanish historians of the Americas as de Landa,[1] Sahagún,[2] and Torquemada[3] are truly remarkable monuments to the beginning of the revolution in religion. For with all their theological presumptions and overall negative evaluations, they were able to perceive positive accomplishment (especially the sophisticated mathematical, astronomical and calendrical structures of the Maya and Aztec) and, most important of all, positive comparison to ancient European-Mediterranean religious elements. Thus we find correlations of similarities in form between Graeco-Roman and Aztec sacred images (primarily cult statuary) and while in many ways simplistic and the consequent theories of mutual origins syncretistic, they were often able to see to some degree beyond the vast differences of cultural style to seek some type of mutual significance between separate traditions. For Renaissance Europeans with all the contemporary value prejudices for the Classical, this was an amazing intellectual accomplishment indeed (especially if we recall the horror of demonism which Aztec religion evoked in the Spaniards, not to mention the simple "ugliness" of any primitive art tradition to the pre-modern Westerner).

With these Spanish historical-cultural accounts the earliest phase of the comparative study of religion begins, ultimately proliferating into a number of historical and empirical disciplines. However, the faltering and somewhat haphazard interests of these Sixteenth and Seventeenth Century inquirers had no immediate effect on European intellectuals (in the main, publication of these early histories came many years later). The absorption of the Indian cultures into the Spanish colonial culture terminated further explorations, and European fascination with its own Graeco-Roman past and with the Far East turned attention away from the Americas for more than two centuries. Seventeenth and Eighteenth Century antiquarians began to evolve a new dimension of insight into Classical religion beyond the literary. At the close of the Eighteenth Century, as antiquarianism mutates into archaeology at Pompeii and Herculaneum and in Egypt after Napoleon, the recognition is made that a religious tradition is not a theological abstraction but is integral to the whole way of life of a people. A dilemma is thus created: the disciplinary character of these new studies necessarily strives toward objectivity, yet from the nature of the traditions as historically *social,* every actual religion must reflect a range of individual experience which cannot be reduced validly to pre-set categories, of whatever origin.

The dilemma becomes practically operative in the later Nineteenth Century with the development of theories of religion. Comparative studies of aspects of religious traditions give rise to the need for comprehensive theories which will account for differences and similarities positively. In 1871, with the publication of *Primitive Culture,*[4] Edward Tylor becomes the father of anthropology (interestingly enough, coming to the general study of human culture through the study of religion in culture), and the anthropology of religion together with the sociology of religion gives rise to a variety of empirical disciplines proper to this field. In 1875 Max Müller undertakes the publication of the *Sacred Books of the East*[5] series, opening up on a large scale the sources of oriental religious thought for the West and calling for a development of a new historico-literary criticism for the positive comparison of the foundations of Eastern and Western religious thought. Reflecting the Nineteenth Century's unlimited confidence in science and objective history, both Tylor and Müller, together with all who followed them, took for granted that the disciplined study of religion would result in the discovery of some single essential structure underlying all the differences. Therefore it was the first task of any objective study to *reduce* the phenomena to this one ultimate system.

Thus, the initial phase of a positive confrontation of religious traditions is ambiguous. On the one hand it marks a radical departure from the older theological interest of one tradition in any other—at best allowing relatively minor accommodations in a process of conversion, and at worst the practical preparation for genocide. On the other hand virtually all theoretical development is reductionist in one way or another. For the first time there is an objective interest in each tradition without theological prejudice for or against any. Yet this objectivity has a purpose not congenial to the actual traditions as these are integrally lived. For some, the objectivity sought was subject to a philosophical or ideological presumption that any religious tradition in itself ultimately was invalid, in terms of a final view of a materialist human nature. Thus, evolutionally each tradition served a transitory function only—now passing away definitively with the advance of Science. For others, the objectivity sought was reductionist in terms of a singularity in religion: the stripping away of "non-essential" differences revealing the inner and commonly shared essence of universal religion—the scientistic adaptation of Rousseau's natural religion of the *homo religiosus.*

The failure of this first phase can be traced to the attempt to solve the dilemma of objectivity-subjectivity in favor of objectivity alone. Any study of religions quickly reveals the fact that no religion exists as a system abstracted from the actual people *who are religious,* and yet these people exhibit commonly shared patterns of religious life—*religious traditions*—which can be spoken of beyond the individuality of each participant. An objective study must account for similarities and differences within the same theory structure, and this makes reductionism impossible. No one is ever observed as a *participant* in "universal religion." No one is ever observed in a pattern of religious activity which can be equated absolutely with some *other* function. Aspects of religious activity may be shared by those in other traditions and hence difference need not preclude similarity. And aspects of religious activity certainly have immediate relevance to other functions (psychological, social and cultural) and hence religious tradition is integrally within the total pattern of living.

The ambiguity of the first phase of positive confrontation includes a special sense of success as well as of failure. For from this point on the previously isolated character of religious traditions is no longer possible. Whatever the limitations of the first theories and the initial understanding of the potentialities of the situation, the transferal of detailed and accurate information about the traditions together with the occasions for actual contact had achieved positive confrontation insofar as interest was now centered upon the traditions as they are. This seems to be a modest accomplishment. But in terms of the long prior history of negative confrontation it marks a revolutionary turning point, coinciding remarkably with the scientific and socio-political dimensions of the general revolution away from the separatist character of pre-modern humanity.

II

Through the long millennia of evolution and cultural development mankind had emerged in separate groupings with multiple traditions whose interrelations were generally oppositive. The self-identity of groups was achieved and maintained through a process of group isolation, with paramount value attached to the sense of "belonging" which, in turn, was both formed by and also itself formed a sense of the alienness of "others." Among tribal peoples it is especially easy to discern how charged with value this identity through separateness becomes, where usually the alien group is not simply "other," but is feared, despised or hated. Thus, for example, the first European contact with various North American Indian nations was often colored by the attitudes of the neighboring tribes previously encountered; one such instance, involving the Dakota nation, is typical of many: the French had heard of the Dakotas through the neighboring

Ojibwa, whose name for the Dakotas (which means *the allies*) was Nadowessioux—the French shortened it to Sioux—meaning *the enemies*. Over and over we find names of alienation imposed on "other people," or their own names taking on meanings of hatred—such as "Jews," "the Turk," "Huns" and so on.

It was not simply the genetic cohesion of the group which was being fostered and protected as a matter of survival. (In fact very often a common ancestry, though highly valued, might merely be putative.) Rather, it was the way of life—the whole pattern of shared values and the sharing of current experiences—which was reinforced by separateness. And of course this includes preeminently religious value and experience, which cannot be dissociated from the rest of culture in pre-modern peoples, and which is their most dynamic center of self-identity.[6] Whether among tribal peoples or those of the great civilizations, the outsider was the barbarian. One might have positive relationships with one or another group, but these were pragmatic in character, even if long standing.[7]

This separation made it possible to keep from any positive evaluation of any aspect of the "barbarians'" way of life. Though Greeks might borrow ideas or technology from their neighbors, how often this is spoken of in myth-symbol as a theft of a treasure or power possessed by the barbarian through some other source (taken originally from the gods, or given by them to the barbarian for him to guard, or the like). The medieval Christian in learning from the Muslim could be certain that the medical or technical item involved had been discovered originally by sorcery. And the Seventeenth Century Chinese were convinced that the ugly Westerners were themselves demons or at least the worst of barbarians descended from demons.

And with religion and the way of life integral in the experience of any people, this negative separatism necessarily made a positive evaluation of religion impossible, even in terms of the most fundamental relationships. Thus for centuries Christians, Jews and Muslims were commonly convinced that the other two worshipped a God other than "their own," and this in spite of a mutually recognized historical relationship. (Needless to say it was also obvious to all three groups together that all other barbarians were still worse, worshipping idols and devils—not even "false gods.") As aliens were termed barbarians culturally, so religiously they were infidels, heathens, idolaters and so on. As a counterpoint within this pattern, conversion from one religion to another inevitably meant a corresponding conversion in culture. (The rise and spread of Islam was also integrally the development and extension of an Islamic civilization; early Chinese and Indian converts to Christianity received not only a Christian baptismal name but a Portuguese surname as well.)

Now and again several previously separate traditions draw together to form a new whole, yet if we look closely we find that this does not break down separatism but actually reinforces it. Thus, the Alexandrian Greek rule throughout the Near East extended Greek culture and religious structure through a process of absorption and syncretism. The one empire Alexander sought to create, embracing both Greek and Persian, was to be dominantly Greek in thought and language. The religious traditions were drawn together by the simple process of giving Greek identity to the "other" cults. The syncretists discovered that the barbarian gods were really the Greek gods in another guise or were further offspring of the original Olympians. And so in Ptolemaic Egypt the Hellenistic statues of the gods wear archaic Egyptian cult symbols on their heads and are called by Hellenized Egyptian names. But the negation of separatism is clearly asserted. If these are *no longer* barbarian it is because they have *become* Greek. The ultimate failure of Alexandrianism in Persia and northwestern India is ultimately the failure of the Greeks to absorb the aliens.

We find this type of pattern repeated often, especially where the practical basis for the attempted unification is the military superiority of one of the participating groups. The last outstanding example is probably that of Akbar (1542–1605), Mogul Emperor of India, who tried to bring religious order to his violently diverse domains through a thorough-going syncretist concordism embracing all the religious traditions he knew of—pleasing none, of course, and earning him the titles of heretic and apostate among his fellow Muslims. Although Max Müller's designation of Akbar as the proto-founder of the study of comparative religion is probably somewhat romantic, the Emperor should be given credit for his insistence that concordism must embrace all traditions without prejudice to any one. At least in this Akbar had gone beyond the imperialist syncretism of Alexander.

There is another and much more important pattern of negative confrontation occurring in pre-modern religion, one which makes a major contribution to the contemporary situation (as well as creates an immense inheritance of problems). Most of the "great religions" have found themselves as direct successors to older traditions, or have absorbed important elements of what theoretically should have remained alien. Consequently they have had to evolve a positive understanding of this process, positive at least in the sense that the area in question was recognizable as having belonged to some other tradition and hence its presence now in both traditions must be justified.

Early Christians "baptized" Socrates, Plato and Aristotle, seeing the philosophers as precursors to the evangelists, preparing the way for the Christian Gospel intellectually among the Greeks. Thus, Justin Martyr breaks down any ultimate barrier between Christian and "non-Christian":

Christ is the *Logos,* in Whom the entire human race has a portion, and all are Christians who have lived according to this *Logos,* even though, like Socrates and Heraclitus among the Greeks, they are accounted godless.[8]

Clement of Alexandria goes further, affirming a direct continuity of Christian wisdom with that of the ancients:

Pythagoras and his disciples and Plato as well followed that inward vision of theirs which was aimed at the Truth, and they did this not without the help of God. And thus in certain things they were in agreement with the words of the Prophets. They searched through Truth in part and in whole, and honored it by the for-

mulations of their thought which were in clear harmony with the
intelligible nature of things, for they had received an intimation
of that which is related to Truth itself. Hence the Greek love of
wisdom is like a lamp whose wick has been lit by men "skilfully
borrowing light from the rays of the sun." Yet it was only when
the *Logos* of God had been proclaimed that the holy light blazed
forth in fulness. From this we see that borrowed light is useful in
the night, but all flames are outshone when it is day: for the
night itself has been made day by the powerful sun of spiritual
light.[9]

This assimilation was taken far beyond a selection of philosophers, however, embracing by implication the whole of Classical
civilization. Thus the Cumaean sibyl became a prophetess fore-
telling the coming of Christ to the Emperor Augustus. A salvific
Providence was seen in the Greek defeat of the Persians and the
Roman defeat of the Carthaginians, and Graeco-Roman polit-
ico-cultural history was seen as the essential vehicle for Christianity.[10] The Christian relation to Judaism was framed more negatively, Christians seeing themselves as the new and true
Israelites displacing the original and now "unfaithful" Israel.
And so Christians were free to take what seemed "true" from the
Judaic Tradition, rejecting everything else as part of old Israel's
"apostasy." In strikingly similar circumstances Islam has done
the same, inheriting the eastern Graeco-Roman philosophical
tradition and chosen elements of Judaism and Christianity.

In every case the same type of value judgment is made. First,
of the now extinct ancient Greeks and Romans, each sees the inherited portions of their new way of life as purified from ancient
barbarism. Next, Judaists classically regard Christians as at best
an heretical semi-gnostic sect of *alien* people (and hence conversion from Judaism must be seen as defection simultaneously from
religious orthodoxy and from one's own people). Christians regard Judaism as truncated, failing of its proper fulfillment and so
as ultimately faithless in all that the prophets had sought to prepare; Christians have an even more negative evaluation of Islam,
regarding it as a somewhat primitive perversion of both Scrip-

tural Judaism and Christianity—whose only truly positive feature is the insistence on monotheism. Finally, Muslims see both Christianity and Judaism as truncations of the final religious fulfillment revealed through Muhammad, and so also as unfaithful to orthodoxy since each had to pervert doctrine to keep from recognizing the completing truth of Islam; in addition there is the dilemma of which is more unfaithful, Christianity which is supposed to be committed to the worship of three gods, or Judaism which rejects Jesus as the greatest of all the prophets of Israel and the precursor to the Apostle.

The Orient provides us with still more examples of this process. Thus, in India commonly Hinduism and Buddhism regard each other as heresies. In China Confucianism benignly allowed for the accommodation of any religious tradition, insisting that all final values rested in the *Way of Ritual* (i.e., Confucianism), itself embodying the Absolute in human relationships; as Confucianism came to permeate all of Chinese culture it mattered little if there were many popular cults (even though Buddhism also bore the opprobrium of being "foreign").

Later European contact with the Eastern Traditions merely complicated this pattern. Ricci, as the first Christian missionary into China, accommodated Confucianism to serve as the vehicle for Christianity—opposing it to Buddhism and Taoism, and choosing from Confucianism elements he could think of as representing a primitive remainder of a revelation given before Noah[11] (rejecting everything else of course as barbaric perversions of the truth by the later Chinese). And Buddhists have accounted for what in Christianity seems close to their tradition by making Christ a Western Buddha—perhaps a fair turnabout for St. John Damascene who heard of Gotama's life and presumed he must be an outstanding early Christian saint of India.[12]

Both syncretism and selective accommodation reflect the tension arising in a separatist context when any awareness of confrontation takes place. The "others" are being accounted for negatively, either directly as heresies and the like, or indirectly when they are "made over" into something which fits the new context. As noted previously, the sense of separation was necessary for group survival, or more positively, self-identity required the assertion of uniqueness so that participants in the culture-religious group could achieve the degree of coherence necessary for survival. Now and again individuals might glimpse something of a further universal significance of the shared values and experience, but there was no practical vehicle to extend the glimpse to full vision, since the vision to be full must itself be the result of sharing—if it is a vision of man socially as well as individually, of man as he actually is.

The problem of separatism has taken on new dimensions in the recent relationships of science and ideology to religion, or, better, to religions. The radical development of complex technology marking the industrial revolution with its massive pattern of socio-cultural change, and then the even more radical development of the new science have both called for an interpretation of the new expansion of the vision of life. The technological and scientific revolutions are the bases of the possibility of the unification (or destruction) of mankind, and yet the first ideological statements have been syncretistic or accommodational, following the older pattern of separatism. Thus, one of the earliest and most influential of scientific theorists on religion, James Frazer,[13] selectively accommodates religious traditions to the new science with the notion that religion evolved in response to the practical failures of primitive magic in its attempt to control the forces of nature, and now science emerges to replace the failure of religion. (Although Frazer's general theory structure of religion is no longer held, the assumptions concerning science as the replacement of religion are strongly entrenched.[14]) Religions are here seen to exist only on an instrumental basis, ignoring the clearly non-instrumental dimensions prominent in every tradition. As the instrumentality of the new science is "more effective," religion is seen as obsolescent superstition. A psychological approach ends similarly, with religions selectively evaluated as fulfilling

needs now better fulfilled psychiatrically (with the analyst replacing the priest). And the major ideologies follow the same pattern of reduction and negative accommodation.

III

As we return to the notion of convergence in civilization we
should be aware of its potential for the religious traditions. For if
concretely any religious way of life is such insofar as it is integral
to the total way of life of any actual people, then the tendency of
the many heretofore separate ways of life to converge toward
some significant unity (with diversity) must involve the following
possibilities. One or more (possibly all?) of the historic religions
will cease to exist. Or, the heretofore separate religions, like their
original cultural matrices, will tend to converge toward a significant unity (again with diversity). Or, the separate religions
will tend to remain separate in spite of the convergence of their
cultural matrices. These possibilities can be interrelated and so
must be explored together, both as to their meaning and their
predictability. (Needless to say, all exploration in this direction
presumes the convergence of civilization as a coming fact—as has
been indicated several times previously—and the characteristic
significant unity remains undefined yet should be sufficiently clear
in intended meaning from the entire context of the discussion of
convergence.)

Any previous culture moving into convergence with others
may undergo such radical changes that the culturally essential
bases of its religious tradition disappear. In such an event the religious tradition as actually lived by the culture group either
ceases (that is, they cease to live it), or new foundations are found
for it whereby it can continue to be lived but, of course, with
modifications. We have been observing a form of this situation
during the last several centuries in the destruction or radical
change of primitive cultures especially under the impact of European colonialism. The gap is so great between the two forms of

the cultures that commonly the primitive religion disappears rapidly. On a level closer to true convergence (rather than the radical acculturation experienced by most primitives) the century of culture change undergone by Japan provides an excellent case history. The opening of Japan to the West in the Nineteenth Century supplied in its first phase a new basis for primitive Shinto. During centuries of dominance by Buddhism, Shinto had been fairly well subordinated and absorbed into Buddhism, having ceased for all practical purposes to have a fully distinct or separate existence. Under the impact of westernization, however, the new nationalism, especially with its potential for imperial expansion, formed a basis for a new Shinto (in the primary form of the cult of State Shinto) effectively cut off from Buddhism and no longer needing the support of the older amalgam. The military collapse of the new nationalism in 1945 brought with it the collapse of State Shinto. While culturally important elements can remain as Japan continues to evolve her new type of civilization, it seems impossible to imagine the formulation of a new Shinto. (The many post-war sects derivative from the older Shinto most probably represent a transitional stage in religious development —*away* from Shinto rather than toward a new Shinto—and, given their socio-economic setting, can be expected to give way to newer forces in the future.)

We should not confine the question to the East or to tribal peoples. Western religions—most of Christianity and Judaism—are keenly aware of the challenge of survival (meaningful, integral survival) in the context of a radically evolving Western culture. Quite apart from the pattern of convergence and the consequent influences coming to bear upon Christianity and Judaism from "outside," Western technological-scientific civilization is involved in so extensive a pattern of culture change as to raise the question of relevance for its traditional religious systems. The resolution of the issue in the West depends on whether the religious traditions can demonstrate a new relevance to the new civilization—whether the religious way of human involvement really matches and is integral to the total way of life. And this new relevance must mean something genuinely new in the religious traditions.

Will all the historic religions "survive" the vast culture change coming with the spread and intensification of the technological and scientific revolutions and with the convergence of civilization? To this there is no empirical answer except to recognize that none can survive unchanged. The degree of change in religions will match the degree of change in the culture traditions which move into unity; the degree of continuing self-identity will match the degree of true diversity entailed in convergent unity. The pattern of change seems to resolve the question of the possibilities open to religion—that the separate traditions either remain separate or correspondingly converge. To put it boldly, can any religious tradition remain separate and survive?

The ultimate factor determining the self-identity and cohesion of any culture group, and hence which stabilizes its way of life, is an ongoing situation of shared experience. The sharing of experience constitutes a group of people to be a community. Language, custom, law and all the other categories are the instruments whereby the sharing takes place. As new experiences originate, ultimately always in terms of individual experiencers, they become culturally significant and part of the society insofar as they are shared. The more kinds of experience there are to share, the more complex the culture and the more sophisticated the instruments of sharing. The complexity and instruments, in turn, condition the participants to seek correlated experiences and to develop the new culture areas as proliferations of the already shared pattern. The historic religious traditions were formed and developed in (relatively) isolated cultural matrices. In a convergent unity of civilization there will be no isolated cultures and hence no experience of general social separation. Can there be any significant separation of religious traditions? If the way of religion and its values and experience are one with the way of life of a people, then a unitive way of life in which historic diversity is no longer separatist simply precludes separatist religion. In terms of the sharing of experience as the ultimate foundation of community, if the experience shared is of a unitive way of life, an isolate or separatist religious experience cannot be shared.

It is here that we must take issue with the previously cited conclusion of Panikkar: "Asian civilizations will continue to develop their marked individuality and *remain spiritually and intellectually separate from Christian Europe.*" If the most extensive sharing of experience does take place, from that point on what would be the positive basis for spiritual and intellectual separation? To equalize the issue (and remove the historic conditioning of anti-colonialism), can Christian Europe remain spiritually and intellectually separate from Asia? Actually the most impressive indication of what is happening even now is provided by the impact of ideological Socialism (a typically European development) upon Asia—certainly China and other Asian states are not remaining spiritually and intellectually separate from Marxist Europe!

Although this begins to reveal the impact of convergence on any religious (and/or ideological) tradition, the issue must be developed within the projected context of the experience of living in a unitive convergence. (And in this projection there is no inclusion of any estimate of when it can take place except "in the foreseeable future".) In a unitive civilization can the geographic designations of "Europe" and "Asia" (or any others) have the same meaning as they do for us at present? Such factors, among many, as immediate and mass communication and the local mobility made possible by mass transportation inevitably will make irrelevant the sense of identification in terms of historic geography. Primitive though the situation still is, we can see an excellent example of this in the rapid decline of regionalism in the United States. A century ago the Civil War was fought bitterly and disastrously on the basis of communities rooted in a geographic sharing of experience: the North *regionally* did not share the way of life of the *South*. Although some regionalism still exists, it is fading rapidly in the face of the educative effects of communication and a constant geographic movement of the population in response to economic change. Thus, apart from short-term movements such as tourism, it is estimated that approximately one-third of all families in the United States change residence each year. Mass communication and the periodic relocation of so many in the population give rise to a new pattern of experience. Life values are no longer *located* in the old manner. A separate culture is no longer identifiable with geographic regions.

Whenever it takes place, a comparable pattern of experience will involve the descendants of the present population of Asia (and, of course, Africa and Central and South America). As for centuries, the overwhelming majority at present live their whole lives in one small region and hence all values, intellectual and spiritual, must be identified with the *place* where experience occurs and is shared. Ultimately, "Asia" and "Europe" will be geographic entities of a new whole, whose population and community will be identified with the whole as such, with a further historic identity through the *process* whereby the unity came into being.

If people begin to experience a positive confrontation of the heretofore separate religious traditions, what will keep them from acting or responding positively? In the past as we know this produced the simplistic and abortive patterns of syncretism, making over what was encountered in terms of what was already positively experienced. Or it could produce conversion to the new and rejection of the old. And so on. But all these are responses conditioned by separatism. The experiencer was seeing the religious way of those "other" people, whose way of life and pattern of experience he did not share. The opposite will be the case in convergence. There will be many varieties—individuals and groups—of "our" people, the only people who exist! If the diversities experienced will now be sensed as necessarily *meaning something together,* then the awareness of religious traditions will call for the development of a *meaning together.* Or structured according to the challenge of relevance, can a religion which remains separate be relevant to a way of life deeply involved in the unitive sharing of what was once separate but which is now the constituting dimensions of a whole?

Without necessarily seeing the positive possibilities as yet, many Christians have begun to face the loss of isolation and with it the loss of security in a self-identity *against* "others." After centuries of mission to convert all non-Christians, and especially after the hopes in this line falsely afforded by colonialism, Christians have been shocked awake to the fact that they are a minority of the total human race and most probably will become proportionately an increasingly smaller minority. But this has been seen only negatively. The fact that there are so many in other religious traditions (especially if we include the newer secular ideologies) and that they are not likely to become Christians, must mean that Christians are supposed to be a separate minority, perhaps forever. From this various theological suggestions are made, most notably the notion of a Christian Diaspora: while cooperating in many spheres of life with the "others," Christians are to constitute a smallish witnessing community (small, but as large as possible!). The Diaspora community is basically withdrawn, set aside, very tolerant of the "others" and even "accounting for them" theologically, but in the last analysis not communicative in the ultimate area of religious values.

However, unless a rigorous and broad pattern of cultural isolation can be provided for the protection of the commitment to separation, such Christian Diaspora communities will have to face a rather quick erosion as the sharing of all other values of the unitive culture challenges the validity of the non-unitive (a somewhat comparable situation which has overtaken contemporary Judaism since the removal of the cultural protection of the old ghetto). For individual Christians will inevitably come face to face with positive values, historically derived from non-Christian sources, and these will be constituting parts of the convergent community at large.

Though the details vary, every religious community is beginning to react to positive confrontation. Panikkar's ideal of spiritual and intellectual separation is the potential of an Indian Diaspora. The dilemma facing Judaism attempting to continue isolated existence and being eroded by secularism is the end-product of a Diaspora culture which finally has collapsed (most evident, paradoxically, in the progressive de-Judaizing of the secularism of the State of Israel).

Except as a desperate hope, there seems to be no positive reason to expect that an isolated religious tradition can continue to exist as cultural convergence takes place. In which case if the historic traditions cannot themselves converge in a manner relevant to the unitive constitution of civilization they must cease to exist.

The consideration of cultural and religious convergence must be disconcertingly general at this point because we simply have not yet had the *experience* of convergence even though we can recognize that it has begun to take place. But we can already know something of the limits and range of meaning involved.

As with general cultural convergence, religious convergence is unitive yet diversified. It excludes reduction and substitution as emerging from the unitive process, expecting, rather, some form of unitive pluralism. Religious convergence is not syncretism: it does not consist in a selection of similarities, reducing the many to one on the presumption that they are nothing more than relatively minor variations of the same reality. Religious convergence is not imperialism: it does not consist in the emergence of any one tradition as simply dominant and absorbing the others, allowing at most a residue of minor variant forms.

The separate traditions arose in separate cultural matrices. A unitive matrix is developing in which the isolated culture complexes will be seen to be meaningful to each other together, not separately. The corresponding religious traditions can be expected in like manner to be discovered to be meaningful to each other together, not any longer separately.

Put in terms of a religious commitment which presumes the meaningfulness of human history, the religious traditions have developed separately and now will continue their development together. They have a *further meaning together* which we had not even suspected. It is not that we will discover that all along they really were all the same. On the contrary, we must expect to find that their differences, so often accentuated oppositively to insure separation, are actually meaningful together, contribute to each other and constitute the new unity out of their diversity.

This is the range of meaning to be explored: the complementing differences as they mean something new together.

THE
SITUATION
OF
THEOLOGY

I

If we expect to go further than predicting a situation of convergence for the historic religious traditions, and setting limits as to what this situation can and cannot signify—unity and diversity, non-imperialism, non-syncretism, non-reductionism, and so on—we must find or devise some system of analysis for the exploration of the constitution of each tradition and for the consequent evaluation of that constitution in the convergent process.

Once again, such an attempt must be justified in terms of the fact that religious traditions are both subjective and objective. No tradition exists abstracted from those actual individuals who participate. Each is an experiencer, and thus the subjectivity essential to religion. But each attempts to share such experience, and hence the objectivity which allows (and forces) us to speak of an identifiable tradition. Any analytical system as such is limited to the dimension of objectivity in religion but must take into account the resultant partial character of every analytical statement. In more recent studies of religion (both historically and

54

empirically oriented) there has been a general fear of anything giving the appearance of abstract system. In many ways this has proved a salutary fear, insisting that we move away from the type of speculation which dominated earlier theorizing. We no longer feel at ease with all-embracing theories which reduce religious traditions to pre-set categories inevitably derived from a relatively narrow spectrum of experience (and very often imposing Western religious or ideological values gratuitously upon the independence of non-Western development).

However, the fear of the abuse of exploration through systematization must not be allowed to impose a restriction on religious study, confining it to the subjective dimension. There is a self-evident limit to the validity of such a judgment as: there are as many Christianities as there are Christians. Hence, with constant reference to the proper dimension of subjectivity we can hope to develop a methodologically valid instrument of systematization for the exploration of the objective dimension.

But if we look closely we will see that the exploration which truly interests us involves still another dimension. We are concerned with convergence, already begun at least rudimentarily but mostly an evolving future condition. We cannot limit our interest in the traditions to their present state nor to the extremely short-range empirical projections of their present state into the near future. For our interest carries us inevitably into the creativity of the traditions or, more properly, into the creativity of the participants as they move into the radically new religious situation. Convergence in the fully positive sense we have been discussing has never happened before and so there is no pattern of previous experience which can affect its significance and form as it takes place. The religious traditions and their participants are going to change to produce a new situation, not at all unrelated to what went before, but genuinely new. In the context of convergence and thus of every other converging tradition, each single tradition will create, drawing upon its own heritage and all those it is coming to share.

This creativity presumes that traditions are historical in a processual sense. That is, their participants are not static, not simply receiving and handing on a religious heritage as a "thing." Rather, the tradition is produced by the participants in a constantly developing process of religious people who experience and share, whose sharing in turn evokes new experience which both recreates something of the former experience and creates something new, and this in turn is shared, and so on. Unless we practice reductionism and identify this process deterministically as the simple and direct manifestation of something else (social, cultural, psychological), the creativity of the experiencing-sharing process must also be accounted for in any systematization. Although this must be discussed at greater length later, it is this creativity which takes place in the religious process which calls for another kind of analysis to complement those made possible by the application of historical and empirical disciplines to the objective "stuff" of religious traditions.

Without attempting to define the term at this point, but simply to indicate something of its intended scope and relation to other disciplinary studies, we will designate the attempt *to analyze systematically the creative process* in any religious tradition as *theology*. Theology in this development must involve the following. First, since its disciplinary purpose is to systematize, it must be oriented to the *objectivity* of a tradition, to the analyzable content of its constitution. Next, the objective dimension must be accepted as *occurring* in subjective experiencing-sharing, and hence always in *immediate positive relationship* with all that the experiencer-sharers are, socially, culturally and psychologically (and therefore theology is necessarily and internally related to the empirical disciplines). Finally, as this religious community individually and together is necessarily *processual,* theology is always involved in and reflective of the *creativity* of the on-going tradition.

In this usage theology differs from historical and empirical disciplines necessarily only as regards its active role in religious creativity. In analyzing religious content and relating a tradition to its total human context, historical, empirical and theological disciplines can achieve a high degree of coincidence, especially methodologically. But the historical and empirical disciplines cannot participate in current-future religious creativity; at most they report it or attempt to predict a portion of it in terms of probabilities. In our issue of convergence, only a theological entrance is possible if we wish to explore "from the inside" of experiencing-sharing what a tradition can create in and for the new situation. For, again, unless we are reductionists, the creativity in religion demanded and allowed for by the convergence of civilization must come authentically from within the religious process.

Admittedly, the use of *"theology"* to designate this area of analytical system is proposed as a development from past usage toward what is felt as necessary for the future. The proposal is not arbitrary, however. It does not seem, for example, that some other or some new term could be used just as well. We will explore this as we attempt to define this meaning for theology in the actual context of the religions which are drawn toward convergence.

We must also seek to relate any new meaning for theology to that which comes from past development. As a term and category of discipline it is proper to the Western experience alone, found only in the Judaic, Christian and Muslim intellectual traditions. There is no category of discipline which directly corresponds to theology native to any religious tradition of the East. Is the term and category, then, an unwarranted imposition of Western values upon the authentic independence of non-Western Traditions? Perhaps the reverse question is just as important: would not the exclusion of theology from the Western Traditions be an unwarranted imposition of non-Western values? Such a conflict in values can only be resolved by a development of theology capable of continuing processually the values of the Western Traditions in convergence with the Eastern, and which does not impose arbitrarily upon the East (and yet which could, and should, stimulate a new level of creativity from within).

We will return later to the consideration of what theology has been for Judaism, Christianity and Islam, especially as this has bearing on what any convergent theology can be for both West and East.[1] But as both an evaluation of past function and potential for the future require some type of norm of judgment beyond the three general characteristics for the scope of theology as suggested above, we must seek at least a working definition of theology. This cannot be drawn simply from past Western experience if we are to be consistent with the openness of the conditions set by convergence. We must begin at the more fundamental level of the historic experience—the situation of theology—and explore the peculiar suggestiveness of the *human situation* as the necessary context in which a *theological process* occurs, and thus occurs with subjectivity, objectivity and creativity.

Situation points toward the human condition, the historic reality of the life-situation of actual men which has given rise to whatever theology is and which remains the norm for judging what it can be. Emphasis on situation will demand that we explore the meaning of theology within the context of its actual occurrence as a phenomenon of human knowing and not as a mere abstraction. Real people have "theologized," and apparently still do. Therefore, our question in seeking the meaning of theology in convergence is not: is theology of any significance? but: what are people doing when they "theologize," what of themselves (at least in part) are they expressing?

If we take the orientation of human situation we will see immediately that in the West theology today is striving to express something of profound significance in man's continuing expansion of his awareness. The entire spectrum of activity which we designate as theology is undergoing internal upheavals of maximum proportions. Some presume these are the death-throes— and among these are what might be called apocalyptic theologians who interpret triumphalistically such developments as the "death-of-God-theology" as signs of the imminent end of the world (for some a periodic hope rather than fear!).

Others see contemporary theological upheaval as in complete continuity with the general crisis in civilization and heralding a radically new beginning in the total human situation.

The issue, therefore, is to come to a definition of theology, not simply as an abstraction but as an expression of the human experience, as reality lived out by actual men, and thus as significant within the context of the contemporary human situation. Further, rooted to this extent and in this manner in man's awareness of himself and his universe, the definition of theology we seek must be extended maximally and not be derived from one tradition of religion or civilization (quite apart from the question of convergence). Therefore, we must turn to the most fundamental observations to be made of actual men to identify factors which would be basic to any theological tradition which could be formed.

The obvious and necessary place to begin is with man himself. Yet most older theological traditions do not begin with man at all, and indeed some seem never to reach man. Man as the beginning point is obvious and necessary only if whatever theology is must be in the human life-situation. Typically, older formulations of the nature and function of theology have presumed that the basic problem is that posed by the affirmation of divinity; the fact of humanity could be taken for granted, often enough because humanity was reduced to an idealization—an ideal human nature was substituted for actual men, as unreal as the "average man" of statistics. Thus the etymological formation of the word "theology" clearly indicates the evaluation of the issues: the central concern is divinity—*theos*—while man, the foundation of the proposed knowing—*logos*—is effectively and rather drastically subordinated. A situational approach to theology must challenge such an orientation. Whatever significance is to be given properly to the *theos*-category, it is the *logos*-category which must occupy first place in our exploration. And this cannot mean that we will be content simply with the pursuit of theories of knowledge. We must ask: what is the significance of *man in the process of knowing?*—the kind of knowing identified by the designation *theology.* The two basic elements, *man and knowing,* demand that any realistic theology be fully grounded in the historic character of the religious tradition. Hence both in content and function the *logos*-category must not be treated as a logical abstraction (and subjected to the mental gymnastics so often indulged in in the past), but must be *located* in the actual process of history.

II

In attempting to deal with the theological situation in terms of historic actuality, we must seek our understanding of the human foundation in a full historic process. What we encounter in contemporary developments is in some sort of continuity with past developments, though of course this continuity may well be characterized as markedly antithetic. The historical perspective is not merely an additional aspect but is an essential factor in our problem, for without it we are not dealing with the actual human situation.

If at all possible we should begin our exploration of theological knowing from outside the Western Traditions. This will enable us to form a preliminary judgment concerning the appropriateness of theologizing in a context of convergence. It can also indicate for the Western experience where convergence in calling for an East-West interrelationship can lead positively. It can test the validity of the presumption that non-Western Traditions in convergence can theologize without this constituting a new imperialism. Therefore, we propose to begin to view the developmental process of theology from a most unlikely historic vantage point, well outside the older Western experience: Confucius.

At first sight, to link Confucius and contemporary theology might seem meaningless (and possibly whimsical), yet if they can be linked validly the combination should produce some unexpected insights. For if Confucianism is properly a religious Tradition and not an ethical philosophy only (as commonly thought of by Westerners), what revisions in the Western concept of religion must be made? If Confucianism theologizes, does this throw light on non-God-centered contemporary problems? Or, if Confucian concern for the values of civilization is properly a theological concern, what does the dichotomous structure religious/secular mean? Other questions of this type could be asked, all illustrating the implications of theology extended to include Confucius.

Whether or not at this stage we could see Confucius as theologizing, there is no doubt that he addresses himself almost exclusively to the problem of man. His concern is not with a theory of man but with man in his real context. Thus, one of Confucius' personal goals, one in which he is to be bitterly disappointed, is to become the prime minister of one of the feudal states and thus be able to put into practice what he teaches. In fact, for Confucius the true teacher, the complete teacher, is one who is able to effect actual change in others, and not remotely through ideas alone but by practical accomplishment. (It is interesting to note in passing the concurrence with the Marxist concept of the theorist, in which philosophy out of the context of socio-cultural action is a self-contradiction.) The inner reason why Confucius insists on the inseparability of thought and action is his recognition of *man as social.*

For the typical Westerner, the phrase *man as social* actually means very little (especially in psychological impact). This is a primary reason why Confucius with his profoundly social orientation is relatively ignored in the West. Over a period of several centuries of revolutionary changes in civilization Western man has lost sight of his very life-situation, and society has become a *mere practical* circumstance of human life in which the individual exists in near isolation, especially with regard to the deepest of human values.

In Medieval Christian spirituality, at least as popularized, we can see the emergence of what will become a continuing pattern of divisive tension between individual and society: the deepest religious relationship is viewed as the individual *alone with God;* Christian theology is conceived of as intellectual preparation of the individual Christian for the achievement of an essentially isolated mystical experience; the Christian Church ceases to be recognized as a body of people constituted by their out-reaching unity and instead becomes a jurisdictional autocracy and a psychologically introverted anarchy of incommunicable personal piety. Renaissance humanism extends this divisiveness further in individualistic intellectualism; Renaissance nationalism and despotism destroys the earlier socio-political patterns of the extended social consciousness called Christendom. And the Enlightenment enthrones individual Reason in that solemn isolation which must denounce all socially shared values and relationships as the ultimate enemies of man, tolerating those imposed by practical necessity in an uneasy coexistence. The present stage of Western Civilization has been formed by a generation raised in the ideals of extreme Nineteenth Century *laissez-faire* individualism, and has produced the paradox of totalitarianism with the one extreme of absolutizing the individual as society (Hitler's *fuehrerprinzip*) and the other of absolutizing society as the individual (the Marxist *collectivity* prepared for by the Leninist *dictatorship of the proletariat*).

Yet in the very crisis of the Twentieth Century we find signs of a new emergence of a social consciousness, still only in its beginnings, but of great potentiality for the future. In the very area thought individualistically sacrosanct heretofore, human moral conscience, we find significant social stirrings. Is there a social responsibility reaching all of us for the murder of millions of Jews? Does such a social responsibility implicate us all in the centuries of exploitive colonialism and imperialism? What is the social responsibility for war and peace, killing and life-giving, enslavement and freedom? Perhaps most significant of all in current Western society is the unrest in the Christian Church with the growing recognition of the absolute necessity for involvement in the total situation of man and a consequent painful judgment against institutional irrelevance.

Rousseau established an irreconcilable dualism of individual and society:

Man's first feeling was that of his own existence, and his first care was that of self-preservation. . . . If we compare the extraordinary diversity which occurs in the education and manner of life of the various classes of men in the state of society with the uniformity and simplicity of animal and savage life . . . it is easy to conceive how much less difference there must be between man and man in a state of nature than in a state of society, and how greatly the natural inequality of mankind must be increased by the inequalities of social institutions.[2]

However recently this characterized the Western attitude, such an evaluation of what the human condition is today is not only meaningless, in its implications it is repulsive. On the other hand, Confucius proposes that the central concept in our understanding of man is *jen*—man related to man, mankind together (expressed in written form by the combination of the characters for *man* and the numeral *two,* hence *man as social*). Although twenty-five centuries, language, civilization and entire life-patterns separate us, we find a responsiveness to his insight. If we are concerned with the human situation, *man as social* is at the center of any valid understanding.

Confucius discovered that he knew nothing at all about man as an abstraction, he could say nothing at all of Human Nature. He also recognized he did not and could not understand the foundation of man's reality, that although he could speak of man and the universe in terms of ultimacy, the Ultimate as such could be named (the Way of Heaven) but could not be known. What Confucius could study and come to know was man as he lived, the works of man. Thus, in the *Analects* we find a disciple saying:

> . . . . We are permitted to hear
> the Master's views on culture
> and the manifestation of *jen.*
> But he will not speak to us at all
> on the Nature of Man
> and the Way of Heaven.
>
> (*Analects,* Book V:12) [3]

Confucius does not deny Human Nature, a real basis for the commutuality of man and for the recognition of that commutuality, nor does he deny the Way of Heaven, the Ultimate of Reality, Ultimacy.[4] Confucius studies man as man manifests himself, the human phenomenon, that which phenomenal knowing is capable of knowing, and he necessarily discovers that individual men are always social.

III

Theology today, or, more properly, current theological systems and traditions are caught in the tensions of contemporary civilization discovering the positive fact of man as social. This will not mean a return to the primitive consciousness of man as almost exclusively social. We cannot expect the reemergence of the archaic orientation of individuality submerged within the consciousness of family, clan, tribe or nation. Although we have many vestiges of this earlier state with us still (and certain of the characteristics of Twentieth Century totalitarianisms may be at least reminiscent of the psychological dominance of group) it does not seem possible that the recognition of the individual self, once achieved, can be eradicated. Rather we seem to be observing the development of a two-fold integrative awareness, both individual and social. This poses the general problem of establishing the means of integrating these two dimensions of consciousness—heretofore we have been witnessing their divisive tension.

This general problem is also a particular problem for theology. All too many theological systems have been structured along lines which have at least tended to overemphasize the individuality of man, even where the religious tradition they seek to represent has a social center. Thus, the typical pre-modern Christian theological system has so downgraded the social character of Christianity that the discovery of the centrality of the *koinonia* comes as a revolutionary shock calling into question the function and relevance of many institutional forms of Christianity. Even for those who recognize the centrality of *koinonia*-awareness, there is the herculean task of transforming their recognition into the awareness, not simply the idea or conceptualization of the awareness. And, still further, there is the corresponding necessity of developing new theological systems as adequate expressions of the awareness.

Other religious Traditions will face the same or related challenges. Although many non-Western Traditions were not seriously affected on the popular level by the development of Western ultra-individualism, nonetheless they are drawn into the general problem of the emergence of the new two-fold individual-social awareness characteristic of the coming worldwide civilization. For some Traditions the issue is actually the reverse of that facing the West, since they must move from a context dominated by social values which allow little place for individuality; for them the tension arises in the increasing discovery of individuality-awareness modifying social-awareness. Still other Traditions are embedded almost completely in language and culture systems which are disappearing with the growth of a more universal civilization, or they are integral to a cosmology or anthropology which must give way to the reconstructed universe of the new science. In these cases the two-fold individual-social awareness of man forms an image of humanity so different from the old that we cannot expect the religious Tradition intimately linked with such an image to survive it.

The emergence of a new human awareness, then, must effect fundamental changes in theological systems as these are the intellectual expressions of religious traditions, and religious traditions necessarily reflect human reality. However, the new human awareness has even wider effects, not simply on particular theological systems but on the constitution and function of theology in general. Particular systems must devise appropriate formulations of relationships expressive of what man is in a religious awareness both individual and social. But, even more profoundly, we must recognize that this type of awareness insists that theology as such come to grips with the reality of actual men as they are and not be content with mankind in general or man in the abstract.

When we deal with man conceived of primarily according to

individuality we inevitably fall into a paradox: individuality, or the basis for it, is of necessity incommunicable—no matter how closely two individuals resemble each other, actually share characteristics, one individual as such is not in any way convertible into another. There is nothing to say about one individual as such which would be significant to another individual as such—we name or identify the individual and that is all. Therefore, we find ourselves actually unconcerned with the real human individuals and instead speak of abstractions, ideal patterns, unreal men. In all of this we soon forget the actual individual men who supposedly preoccupy us from the beginning. Theology structured according to radical individuality inevitably goes to extremes both ludicrous and horrifying—thus, classic Western scholasticism, concerning itself with "universals," could produce such elusive concepts as *dogness* to categorize the nature of dogs, and Nazi racist ideology with the absolutized individuality of the *fuehrerprinzip* could produce the anti-human concept of the *Untermensch* to render real human beings unreal and hence objects of liquidation rather than murder.

When we deal with man conceived of primarily according to society we fall into the same paradox but with the context reversed: society conceived of as apart from real individuals does not exist, nor can there be any social awareness except insofar as individuals who are conscious succeed in finding ways to share or intercommunicate their separate consciousnesses. There is no one to whom one can say anything about society if the individual is not addressed, and whether each individual is addressed singly or simultaneously with others each must be addressed or none is. Therefore, in a primarily social orientation we find ourselves actually unconcerned with society as it really is and instead speak of something composed of non-individuals, which thus is not composed of men at all and so cannot be real society. The self-contradiction of a theology structured according to society as an abstraction is well illustrated by the concept of the Marxist *collectivity*, a society to be produced by the self-contained dynamics of the dialectic process of history but which will have no significant individuality within it and hence will destroy the dialectic process and become static, futureless and absolutely opposed to the immutable laws which are to create it, a human society without real humans, that is, without humans as we experience them— the only kind we know and thus the only kind about whom we can speak meaningfully.

If theology is to be situated in the actual condition of man and if the *logos*-category of theology is to reflect adequately man's experience in knowing, then the central recognition of theology must be *jen:* man both individual and social, man communicating, man in an ultimately significant relationship. Thus, seen from this orientation theological knowing does not consist in abstract formulas, whatever their derivation, but rather must be the meaningful analysis of the truly significant relations of human experience. Such an orientation in no way compromises the actual commitments proper to any religious tradition. As a system of analysis theological knowing can be developed around any tradition of human experience. If for example the experience occurs because of the manifestation of divinity—revelation—that experience as it occurs in man must have proper human significance both individual and social, and hence at least something of it must be communicable. The development of a theological system takes place in response to the attempt to come to grips with the experience in every communicable dimension.

In the *logos*-category theological knowing is always the same as the attempt to analyze and thus communicate actual religious experience. Differences occur in terms of the content of the experience, the type of effect the experience has upon the individual and hence upon his communication group. The variety in theological systems is expressive of the variety of approach made historically to the content of the *theos*-category. In the study of specific religious traditions the content of the *theos*-category is determined and articulated according to the insight of communities sharing concrete commitments. However, for theology in general an understanding of the *theos*-category cannot be attempted in terms of one specific religious tradition. Yet it is the *theos*-category which specifies theology as a particular kind of knowing, which attempts to analyze and systematize a particular kind of human experience.

Returning once again to our first emphasis, that is, theology in terms of the human situation, a significant functional relationship for the *theos-* and *logos*-categories can be established in the very process of theological knowing. The Confucian concept of *jen* focuses attention on religious experience as both individual and social. However, against our usual Western tendency, *jen* insists that we see the experience as a basic interhuman relationship rather than as an isolatable phenomenon of consciousness. In other words, conscious religious experience occurs insofar as a fundamental human relationship exists which constitutes man what he is. This relationship not only allows for communication, it makes communication inevitable. Thus, a knowing process of analysis, systematization and articulation is integrally part of what it means to be human.

As Confucius observes man actually living out this process he finds that there is something about it which extends beyond momentary experience, transitory relationships, and the simple appearance of things. *Jen* expresses a necessary relationship which constitutes the very condition of human existence and also expresses the further significance of man and his world. Man is constituted in an all-embracing relationship of individuals and this relationship is definitively significant in the most profound sense.

In any theological system or approach to the meaning of theology in general we can recognize that the *logos*-category expresses a definitiveness for man somehow located in the *theos*-category, however the content of the latter may be conceived. Although a theological system may be primitive, poorly systematized and badly articulated, it never fails to express a call for commitment. Theological systems are never indifferentistic theories of religious knowledge. They come into existence for the very purpose of formulating an understanding of religious conviction so that commitment can be specified and made concrete and practical.

It seems clear that one of the basic reasons why the *logos*-category should always be social in its extension is that the human experience in religion always has a characteristic absoluteness about it and hence cannot be confined to the individual without self-contradiction. The urge to communication which gives rise to concrete theological systems is not simply the result of gregariousness or of the psychological need to stimulate others to pursue common interests. The religious experience seems always to insist upon an absolute involvement of everything which actually constitutes man, and hence man's social situation precludes a purely individualistic significance for religion. Thus, theological systems inevitably express involvement of man in the broadest possible terms, reflecting an irreducible human interrelationship which somehow has ultimate significance.

THE
DYNAMICS
OF
THEOLOGY

I

The *theos*-category is the structural element in theology in which concrete conceptualizations of the ultimacy in the religious relationship are attempted. The various theological traditions differ radically in the conceptualizations proposed for the *theos*-category. However they are in complete agreement in the general affirmation that there is a basis in reality for the definitiveness experienced in the religious relationship.

Although it is true that theological systems typically specify a conceptual content for the *theos*-category, even the slightest acquaintance with the historic religious traditions reveals an apparent contradiction. For while each system does propose a *theos*-category conceptualization, at the same time each inevitably asserts that that which constitutes this category is in itself absolutely unknowable, and thus ineffable.

The oldest texts of Confucianism affirm over and over the paradox of man in a definitive relationship which orients him to an unknowable. Confucius sees man and everything which man

70

does as immediately reflective of the Principle or *Tao* of existence. But although this direct reflectivity of things manifests the *Tao,* the *Tao* in itself remains unknowable. And so Confucianism concentrates man's attention upon what can be known: the outward appearance of things, on-going human relationships and the works of man. But this is not simply a devotion to culture or an ethical discipline; by involvement with all that can be known man can reach the unknown—a harmony of life lived here and now is the mysterious image of a total Harmony in all of reality.

Hence when Tzu-kung says,

> . . . we are permitted to hear
> the Master's view on culture
> and the manifestations of *jen.*
> But he will not speak to us at all
> on the Nature of Man and the Way of Heaven . . .[1]

we are being told two things. First, the Way, or *Tao,* of Heaven and the ultimate significance of man are unknown. But second, to know human culture and the manifestations of *jen* is to reach into the ultimate mystery of man and *Tao.*

Another important text of the *Analects* points up Confucius' recognition of the paradox:

> Someone asked the meaning of the Great Sacrifice.
> The Master said: I do not know.
> Anyone who knew its meaning
> could deal with all that is under Heaven
> as easily as he could look at this
> (and he pointed to the palm of his hand).
> (Book III:11) [2]

The central concern of Confucius as a scholar and teacher was the study of culture and the manifestation of *jen.* For him the most important subject of study was the complex of ritual and ceremonial whereby human relationships, and hence man himself, were most formally expressed. Outstanding among the cultural rituals was the Great Sacrifice which summed up all that constituted society through the affirmation of the continuity of the human community in spite of the barrier of death. The Great Sacrifice ritually united ancestors and descendants in the timeless mystery of family. Yet Confucius cannot say what the inner meaning of the Great Sacrifice is. It is not simply that he does not know. Rather, as the central image of man in his ultimate relationship, the meaning of the Great Sacrifice is the ultimate meaning upon which all of reality is founded. It is the *Tao*, the Principle of Reality Itself.[3] And this in the religious experience of Confucius is completely unknowable.[4]

There is a peculiar subtlety in the thought of Confucius, especially if we view him as theologizing. The *theos*-category is recognized as unknowable and Confucius never is tempted to propose any concrete conceptualization for it. He identifies it, affirms it, and recognizes its absolute significance for all that he does attempt to know. The only positive identification he can give it is as the *Tao*, the Principle. And though the *Tao* can be recognized as expressive of transcendence, as Principle it is always within human reality where it is to be known and followed.

This designation affirms that there is a further significance for the *logos*-category beyond the mere description of human activity. Confucius sees the destiny of each man in the achievement of harmony with other men through life in accordance with the essential social condition of human relatedness, and this human harmony extended to the cosmos which it mirrors. This complete harmony of the *logos*-category, both knowable and achievable, is the image of a further Harmony, the foundation of all reality, which can be reached but which must remain a mystery.

In terms of theology, Confucius starts with man and remains with man—yet this is expressive of a mysterious ultimacy which exceeds what man is and what man does but which gives all that is human a value beyond the passing moment.

In Taoism China gives us another outstanding example of the attempt to formulate man's significance in the religious experience. While Confucianism concentrates on the *logos*-category in its full social extension, Taoism attempts to look within the individual consciousness to discover what happens to man that makes him commit himself absolutely. While highly individualistic, Taoism is nonetheless not anti-social for it presumes that all men have a common origin and destiny though each must walk the path of return alone. Taoism concentrates on the paradox of individual mysticism. To pursue the *Tao* as the Principle of Reality one must wait for it rather than seek it, be quiet rather than active, and prefer unknowing to knowing. Thus, in Chapter 47 of the *Tao Te Ching* we read:

> Without going outside his door,
> one understands everything under the sky.
> Without looking out from his window,
> one sees the *Tao* of Heaven.
> The farther one goes out from himself,
> the less he knows.
> Therefore the sages achieved their knowledge
> without travelling,
> gave the right name to things
> without seeing them,
> and accomplished their ends
> without any purpose of doing so.[5]

Taoism does not look to things for the manifestation of *Tao*, but calls upon the individual consciousness to empty itself so that the *Tao* can fill it in the situation of personal mysticism. As with Confucianism, the *Tao* is always within man and thus the mystical experience must always be a paradox and so must always be expressed paradoxically. Taoism constantly views the human commitment to ultimacy through a symbolic reversal of value. We see this in the water image of the Taoist mystics. In contrast to the heat of the sun and the force of the wind which seem to dominate the world, it is water flowing into the crevices of stone that has the irresistible power when it freezes to break apart the earth and split open mountains. And the Taoist mystic asks what constitutes the usefulness of a bowl—is it its solid sides and bottom or is it the interior emptiness which waits to be filled?

In seeking to express what man is, Taoism is not concerned

with impotence, inaction or passivity. Rather, it affirms that all that is apparently negative is actually positive: the mysteriousness of Reality, intensely active and powerful. Though we seek the *Tao* outside, we will find it only within.

Confucianism sees man and his works as manifesting the ever mysterious *Tao* which remains behind them at their foundation. Taoism attempts to look within, directly at the mysterious foundation. Hence Taoism accepts what man is and what man does, but is only interested in the reversal of all this. Yet, however much Taoism may stress the immediacy of the ultimate Principle to man, it nonetheless affirms that the *Tao* remains unknowable. Thus, Chapter 1 of the *Tao Te Ching* opens with the mysteriousness of the *Tao:*

> The *Tao* that can be trodden
> is not the enduring and unchanging *Tao;*
> the name that can be named
> is not the enduring and unchanging Name.[6]

Chapter 14 provides us with an extraordinary insight into the Taoist coordination of the function of the *logos*-category and the *theos*-category. What is the mystic doing as he approaches the unknowable *Tao* in the situation of human consciousness, what understanding is there and hence what human communication can take place?

> We look at it
> and we do not see it,
> and we name it "the Equable."
> We listen to it
> and we do not hear it,
> and we name it "the Inaudible."
> We try to grasp it
> and we do not get hold of it,
> and we name it "the Subtle."
> With these three qualities
> it cannot be made the subject of description
> and hence we blend them together
> and obtain the *One.*[7]

The same chapter later refers to the *form of the Formless,* the *semblance of the Invisible,* the *Fleeting,* and the *Indeterminable.*

Although Taoism as an experiential mystical process reverses the evaluation of man made by Confucius, they share the same problem when the attempt is made to determine what it is that makes the religious relationship somehow ultimate and definitive. Even diametrically opposed visions of man and hence of the *logos*-category allow for no difference in the attempt to give content to the *theos*-category. The category is affirmed and it is affirmed as profoundly significant for man. Man's relationship to it is seen as real in every sense. Yet, whatever words are used to designate the *theos*-category and however much they may seem to give positive conceptual content to it, it is declared to be simply unknowable, a complete and permanent mystery.

II

As we extend our range of comparison further to observe the occurrence and treatment of the paradox in other areas of major religious development, we find a consistent similarity in the articulation of the basic problem. Whatever the conceptualization of man and the phenomenal universe, and whatever meaning the particular religious tradition gives for man involved in the religious relationship, the "theological" systems as the formal articulations of the religious traditions uniformly assert the ineffability of the *theos*-category. If we look to the development of the two major religious Traditions of India, Buddhism and Early and Later Hinduism, we find two closely related yet quite distinct approaches to the formulation of the paradox.

The religious Traditions of India embrace a vast diversity of developments extending uninterruptedly over four millennia. Together with Hinduism and Buddhism, and the smaller Jainism and Sikhism, India has been the seed-bed of a number of distinctive traditions, and these, in turn, are subdivided into seemingly countless sects and schools of interpretation. The stream of Indian religions arose in the fusion of the Aryan conquerors with the pre-Aryan peoples in the Second Millennium B.C., and the modification of the Aryan way of life as it moved away from the nomadic to the sedentary agricultural pattern already established in Northern India in the region of the upper branches of the Indus River. It was the period of the oral composition of the great body of Vedic literature, finally reduced to written texts about the Eighth Century B.C. The Vedic period embraced the foundation of a new civilization and its heroic age, and it also set crucial lines of thrust for all the future growth which can be identified with orthodox Hinduism. Carried forward in the next century with the rise of the early caste structure as the underpinnings of the new socio-religious system, Brahmanism (as the designation of the early religion) began an era of wide-ranging philosophical and religious speculation identified with the composition of the *Upanishads*, a corpus of varied texts addressed to the experience of reality—what is it? what is the cosmos? what is experience, real or illusory? what is man?

With all the diffusion and subtlety of the Upanishads, all their different interpretations of the things of the cosmos and of man, they agree on one central principle: the real is ultimately unitary, one, wholeness, beyond division or particularity or limited individuation. If we seek a motif to typify the difference between the main thrust of Hinduist thought and that of the West, it would be the overriding sense of the unitive. Generally speaking, Hinduism characteristically takes for granted that, whatever the conceptualization of it, reality is self-evidently One Whole, whereas the West typically is always searching for a sense of wholeness. (It is paradoxical indeed that the Indian Tradition, so unitary-conscious, should exhibit such a tolerant internal pluralism, while Western Traditions, so intent on a quest for unity, should be so insistent on uniformism!)

The Upanishadic drive is not only toward the affirmation of experienced oneness, but toward the interiority of that experience, and hence there is an inherent tension between subjectivity and objectivity, and a variety of often conflicting resolutions are proposed. For the most part the Upanishads favor a monistic position: there is but one actually existing reality, most commonly called *Brahman* (a neuter word, in its older Vedic setting referring to the sacred power of prayer). Brahman is variously conceived— a kind of deity, personalized or not, or a principle, the non-personal matrix from which the universe arises and to which it returns. Brahman is all that is objective, but as the One Real, is also all that is subjective. In Brahman are conjoined the outward world of objects and the inward world of self-consciousness. In the *Brihad-Aranyaka Upanishad* Brahman is identified as the reality within the sun, moon, the heavens, space, fire, water, wind, everything, summed up in the affirmation: "He is their Reality." [8] But Brahman is also the inner center of consciousness within any individual, and the very "soul" of man, the inner selfhood, is itself The One, the *Atman*. Against the popular assumption of the simple individuality of selfhood and hence of the atman as an individual soul, the *Brihad-Aranyaka* asserts there is complete identity between Brahman and Atman: "He is your soul." [9] The true self, atman, of an individual man and the universal self or world-soul, *paramatman*, are one and the same. The *Chandogya Upanishad* proclaims it in the formula *tat tvam asi,* "That art Thou." [10] Brahman is the objective One-All, and is identical with the Atman as the subjective Self of each individual—the only Brahman-Atman, the wholeness of the objective-subjective of Reality.

Yet there is no unanimity among the Upanishads on this apparently monist doctrine. The later Vedantic school will carry the Brahman-Atman monism to its most rigorous conclusion, asserting only Brahman-Atman is in any way real and phenomenal individuation is a pure illusion, but other schools will reject a full monist position and seek another understanding for the unity sensed in the subject-object tension. From the point of view of the West, however, whether or not a fully monist stance is taken by this or that school, the overriding sense of the Wholeness of Reality is integral to Indian thought and so also is the sense of subjective consciousness. Post-Upanishadic schools diverge on the interpretation of subjectivity, but philosophical and religious thought are never simply object-oriented as in most of the West: it is not that-out-there, but *tat tvam asi*, that-within.

Upanishadic subject-object wholeness inevitably concentrated attention on the process of *knowing*, not simply discursive reasoning but depth-experiencing. Later Upanishadic writers used the analogy of dreamless sleep for the kind of consciousness of Oneness to be experienced: if *somehow* the selfhood of the experiencer is in unlimited union with the Atman that is Brahman, then depth-consciousness must transcend the sense of subject-object separation. This is the highest state of mind, the purest moment of the soul, when Brahman-Atman are/is perceived as indistinguishable.

It is evident that any monist or near monist interpretation of the Brahman-Atman unity must deny the possibility of conceptualizing what it is that constitutes the One Real. The capacity to use analogies breaks down internally if the meaning of any individuation is ultimately the same identical meaning of the One. The non-monist interpretations also fail in an attempt to construct a proper concept for the Real insofar as the highest state of consciousness, the depth-knowing of the Real, is not capable of maintaining a subject-object awareness. Thus, whether or not interpreted monistically, the main thrust of Upanishadic thought demands recognition of the *theos*-category as ineffable, while at the same time insisting that whatever does constitute this category it is actually experienced existentially in human consciousness.

The recovery of later Hindusim, after the revolutionary rise of Buddhism and Jainism, centers upon the development of a new factor in popular religion: salvation or liberation through the Way of Devotion, *Bhakti*. Bhakti is the overwhelming sense of loving devotion directed to deity in response to the promise of salvation from the endless round of reincarnation (liberation from the meaninglessness of an apparently isolated infinite series of successive individual existences). The most important text teaching the doctrine of bhakti, one of the sacred classics and one which has influenced virtually all of later Hinduism, is the *Bhagavad-Gita,* the *Song of the Lord.* Composed somewhere near the First Century A.D., the *Bhagavad-Gita* is eclectic in character, attempting to unite the older notions of salvation—the Way of Works (the moral-ethical fulfillment) and the Way of Knowledge (the Upanishadic emphasis on the cultivation of depth-conscious-ness)—with the Way of Devotion. The text never resolves the in-terpretive problem of the Brahman-Atman Oneness, though the monist or near monist emphasis is given greatest prominence, and it leads to at least a partial integration of monist and per-sonal theist understandings of the Sacred.

Returning again to a key differentiation between Indian and Western religious thought, for the West generally, *the first emphasis* is on individuation which, while not in any way denying the uni-tive, insists that the experience of reality is primarily evaluated from the experience of phenomena, individually. For the Indian-influenced East generally, *the first emphasis* is on unity which, while not in any way denying the individual, insists that the ex-perience of reality is primarily evaluated from the experience of "some wholeness" which is "beyond" or "behind" or "within" the phenomenal. A most important consequent of this difference in fundamental orientation is the general tendency in the West to seek the formulation of the experience of Ultimacy in terms of an Ultimate Entity, or Being, or concrete Force or the like (whether or not these are further seen as personal), and in the East to seek the formulation of the experience of Ultimacy in terms of Ulti-mate Truth, or Principle, or Law.

The religious Traditions of India, therefore, must face prob-lems not in the Western experience as they approach the reli-gious issue of the full significance of man, and hence as they ap-proach the "theological" issue of the conceptualization of the *theos*-category. All of Indian thought influenced by the structure of relationships given in the *Bhagavad-Gita* proposes that man's significance is not to be found in the self-which-he-seems-to-be, nor in the world-in-which-he-seems-to-exist, but in One Abso-lute, the Only Real, that which alone can be the True Self, the totally singular unity opposed to the multiplicity of apparently unrelated things.

There is a wide range of interpretations of how this disposition of real-and-illusory is to be understood. Thus, one can see the contrast between the "True Self" and the illusory self as psychological, that is, the "True Self" is the individual as he is actually and not just as he seems to be in terms of personality or the like; paradoxically, in this understanding only individuation is real. Hence the *Bhagavad-Gita* relates easily to various ultra-materialist and atheist schools of interpretation. In what might be seen as a middle range would be schools asserting the interdependent reality of individual, phenomenal selves and the reality of an (entitive) Ultimate Real, either personal or impersonal. And at the other end of the range of interpretation would lie the various monistic schools, most notably the *Vedanta* which has tended to dominate Hinduist thought during the last several centuries. But whatever the school we observe, the *formal structure* True Self/apparent self, Real/illusory, creates the same content problem for the *theos*-category in coordination with the content of the *logos*-category.

Later Hinduist orthodoxy (that is, traditions accepting the inspiration and normativeness of the *Vedas* and the appended *Brahmanas* and *Upanishads*) is represented in six principal schools, other lesser schools being subsumed under these.

The *Nyaya System:* concerned with logic and epistemology, concluding that salvation is achieved through correct knowledge which dispels the false knowledge that is the source of all that is metaphysically false.

The *Vaisheshika System:* a logic of the external phenomenal world, seen as self-existent and formed of atoms in constantly altering combinations taking place under the invisible power of deity, the eternal Soul, the source of individuated souls.

The *Sankhya System:* an atheistic and dualistic interpretation positing two always existing categories, matter and soul (*prakriti* and *purusha*); souls are totally individuated, there being no unitary Brahman-Atman All-Soul; salvation is achieved through recognition that the individual soul is completely uninvolved with matter.

The *Yoga System:* a mental discipline supportive of the Way of Knowledge, the psychological complement to the metaphysics of liberation in the depth-consciousness resolution of subject-object tension.

The *Purva-Mimansa System:* an anti-speculative interpretation of the Vedas as literally inspired and ultimately uncreated texts containing all of the *Dharma,* or truth/law/duty, for man's salvation (the Dharma as the Transcendent Itself, or as the divine offspring of the Ultimate Being).

The *Vedanta System:* radical monism, as developed by Sankara ("non-dualist illusionistic monism," Brahman alone exists, all else is pure illusion), or Ramanuja ("qualified non-dualism," the Ultimate is personal and manifested through dependent individuals who are drawn into union with him as their final destiny), or Madhva ("duality," monotheism with fully distinguished individuals and phenomenal existence).

For our present purposes the exploration of a monist interpretation of the structure True Self/apparent self, Real/illusory, will be the most significant, since the situation of the middle range schools is ultimately comparable to what will be considered in examples drawn from the West, and the situation of the apparently atheist or non-theist schools is ultimately comparable to corresponding Western atheist or non-theist ideologies as "para-religions."

In a monistic reading of the *Bhagavad-Gita* the significance of the religious relationship is conceived of as the One Unmanifest Real being manifested through many appearings which precisely as "manifestings" are not separately the Real. That which appears, which is manifested, is the only Reality existing, and insofar as the various appearances are seen to differ these individuations are illusions and cannot be the Real. It is not that appearings do not happen. That which appears is consistently the One Reality while the many ways of appearing are outside that Reality. This religious tradition draws upon many elements in its attempt to express the proposed relationship between the manifest and the Unmanifest. Mythological figures from the prehistoric era come to constitute a rich variety of vehicles for the symbolization of the Absolute. The One Real is thereby personified in many different ways, expressive of the many types of response made by man to the life situation. Abstract philosophical elements provide another form of expression outside of the context of cultic involvement. Other elements drawn from the experience of mysticism allow for an approach through the most impressive phase of personal consciousness in spite of the characterization of consciousness as illusory.

Yet with all the varieties of expression, the Tradition consistently undercuts any attempt to resolve the paradox of ineffability. Perhaps the most eloquent example of this to be found in the *Bhagavad-Gita* is the presentation of the two visions of the Absolute. In one vision the Absolute is presented in images of splendor, majesty and awe. He is glorified by a series of comparisons in which the greatest things known to man, the most beautiful and pleasing aspects of existence are made the bases for divine analogies. In each instance, however great or beautiful the object is for man, the Absolute is proclaimed still greater, still more beautiful. The second vision of the Absolute is a total reversal of the first. In place of the images of beauty and inspiring glory, the Absolute appears in a nightmare of horror, repelling the terrified beholder. We see the image of a fire-breathing monster with blazing eyes, jagged teeth and tusks dripping with blood, hundreds of hands reaching out for victims who are thrust into the awful mouth and whose flesh sticks between the teeth of the divine destroyer. These two totally contrasting visions presented one after the other lead the beholder dramatically into the paradox of ineffability. Both images are drawn from human experience: man's fulfillment and man's nightmare. These are images of man, and as man himself is unreal the images must be illusions. Whatever the manifestation may seem to be, the Unmanifest must remain unmanifest.

The *Bhagavad-Gita* clearly affirms the paradox in a statement reminiscent of Taoism:

One looks upon It as a wonder;
another speaks of It as a wonder;
another hears of It as a wonder;
and even after having heard of It
no one really does know It.
(Chapter II)[11]

And to prepare us for the understanding of the two visions as the contradictory symbol of the paradox, the Absolute is addressed as Divinity:

You only know Yourself by Yourself.
(Chapter X)[12]

Perhaps the most forceful statement of ineffability is made in Chapter VIII, where the conceptual structure of manifest-and-unmanifest itself is broken through, comparable to the existential breakthrough demanded psychologically by the tension of the two visions:

But beyond this unmanifest there is yet
another Unmanifest, the Changeless,
which does not perish when all beings perish.[13]

Whether or not one follows a monistic interpretation of the manifest-and-unmanifest structure, it is clear that the "something else" or "somehow beyond" of this passage (which is crucial and not simply incidental to the development of thought in the *Bhagavad-Gita*) insists on the affirmation of Ultimacy and in a way precluding any conceptualization except by way of thorough-going contrast.

III

Buddhism comes as a revolution in Indian religion, breaking with the Vedic tradition and the just-formed Upanishadic interpretations. The speculations and introspective character of the

Upanishads had resulted, in part, in a popular sense of negativism and pessimism. If a monist or near monist doctrine were realistic, then the authenticity of individuality was severely undercut. True, the assertion of *tat tvam asi* could be exalting, the "individual" discovering his actual identity to be none other than that of Brahman: I am myself the Only Real. But it also totally depressed what the personal values of the individual could be, rendering them ultimately meaningless. The person in his self-reflectivity was doomed to a thorough-going psychological frustration. Projected into an overall metaphysics of history, the falseness of individuation with its inherent devaluation was magnified infinitely by the presumption of the endless cycle of reincarnation. Through the inexorable effects (*karma*) of what the apparent individual did during his life, the fact and form of his next phase of existence was determined; and the karma of that next life in turn determined the next, and so on in an infinite series with no beginning or end. The prospect of existence continuing after death, thus, was seen as a curse rather than a blessing, symbolized by an always-turning wheel from which there seemed to be no release.

The historic Buddha addressed himself to the existential problem as a psychological reality created by the radical devaluation of the individual and the total pessimism of the meaning of life as endless frustration. Unlike the condition of later Hinduism, Indian thought in the Sixth Century B.C. had not yet hardened around the Vedas, the early caste system and other institutions of orthodoxy, so Gotama was socially free to strike out on a new path. He rejected the relevance of both the ancient teachings of the Vedas and the speculations of the Upanishads, at least for his time and the moment he had to face in attempting to pierce through the seeming meaninglessness of life. He regarded the conflicting views of the more than seventy schools of metaphysics as at least useless for the task at hand. The existential issue was not metaphysical but psychological.

As noted previously in the brief consideration of Hinduism, one marked contrast between Western and Indian thought can be located in the general Western tendency to give first emphasis

to Being or Existence and the general Indian tendency to emphasize the consciousness of the True. Thus, if the Western religious
Traditions have been preoccupied with Ultimate Being (He-
Who-Is, the Creator, Ruler of the Universe, the Supreme Being,
and so on), Buddhism from the beginning has been preoccupied
with Ultimate Truth or, more properly, with the Ultimately
True. One of the fundamental categories of Indian thought is
Dharma, a term which covers a complex of meanings: Dharma
embraces religion in its observances, law, good works, duty, right
and justice, piety, morality, all that in any way is true. With the
emphasis on truth/law in Buddhism, dharma is the universal
principle of existence, the principle of righteousness and morally-
charged action, and, supremely, the Doctrine of the Buddha.
Dharma as Doctrine is not so much *dogma* as *path* of experience; if
one lives by the Dharma he comes to salvation, but the Dharma
must be discovered in the process of seeking perfection, in the actual doing. Hajime Nakamura notes that the Western counter-
part of dharma is the Platonic and Christian-Neoplatonic *logos*,
yet the Eastern dharma tends to be subjective in human behavior
while the Western logos tends to be objective as a principle con-
trolling the world in which men live.[14]

In putting aside all interest in speculative metaphysics, the
Buddha was seeking the Truth of the dilemma of existence so
that an existential solution could be achieved. He was thus concerned with Dharma in the sense of *what is Ultimately True, True* in
that it could be actually experienced and *Ultimately* as reaching
into the fullness of Reality. The starting point of the quest is a
thoroughly pessimistic view of life as meaningless misery, but the
fact that a quest for liberation is undertaken is an affirmation of
an overriding optimism. In the opening sermon of his ministry,
the Buddha establishes the core of all Buddhism in the recitation
of his own experience of liberation. Having tried and rejected the
two extremes of the negation of asceticism and the commitment
to self-indulgence, he has achieved Buddhahood—the fully experienced salvation/liberation of enlightenment—by following the
Middle Path of the Way of Knowledge. The essential Dharma of

Buddhism is summed up in the *Four Holy Truths:* all experienced existence is misery and suffering; the cause of this is in the craving for selfhood satisfaction; suffering will cease when such craving is stilled; this can be done by following the Middle Way, the *Noble Eight-Fold Path*—the cultivation of right views, right aspirations, right speech, right conduct, right livelihood, right effort, right mindfulness, and right contemplation. The fulfillment of the Eight-Fold Path by actual experience results in complete and final liberation, the transformation of existence into the state of *Nirvana,* Changelessness.

Early Buddhism quickly developed a number of interpretive schools, generally divided into *Mahayana* (Great Vehicle), and *Hinayana* (Small Vehicle) or more properly *Theravada* (Way of the Elders). Mahayana Buddhism in its spread through central Asia, China and Japan developed many diverse forms, adapting effectively to differing cultures and older religious traditions; it became concerned with metaphysical speculations, the incorporation of mythologies, elaborate cultic rituals and like matters not addressed by earliest Buddhism. In its most exotic form Mahayana Buddhism gave rise to the Tibetan amalgam of Buddhism, Tantrism and primitive shamanism, *Lamaism* or, more properly, *Vajrayana* (Thunderbolt Vehicle). The various schools differ radically on many central issues, and so there are traditions that are atheistic (at least depending on how theism is defined), theistic— both personal and non-personal—polytheistic, agnostic, and so on. But constant throughout all of Buddhism is the essential Dharma of the Four Holy Truths with the Noble Eight-Fold Path and liberation and Nirvana.

The most concise definition of Nirvana is *the end of becoming.* Crucial to the vision of the Buddha is the experience that the only realistic thing we can say of phenomenal existence is that it is *transitoriness,* a constant process of coming into being and going out of being in an infinite series of rebirths. This is the reason for misery and suffering, and the reason why the experience of suffering reveals to the realistic man that suffering is the very nature of what seems to be so substantial—the universe, life, self.

The noted Ceylonese Buddhist scholar, G. P. Malalasekera, writing as President of the World Fellowship of Buddhists for the 2,500th anniversary observance of the beginning of Buddhism, provides us with an exposition of the core of *Buddha Dharma* in *The Buddha and His Teachings,*[15] prepared especially as an interpretation for the West.

1. *Phenomenal Existence, Samsara, as Suffering/Transitoriness*

"Come," says the Buddha to His disciples, "lead the good life"; and for what end? The extinction of suffering. It would be wrong to think that the suffering which the Buddha envisages is something apart from the ordinary sorrows and pains of life, the trivial material and moral suffering we all know. . . . It is precisely of the suffering we are familiar with that He spoke: old age and illness, death, association with those we dislike and separation from those we love. Nothing can be simpler than this. The Buddha takes His stand upon common experience, on the bitter consciousness of the ills that flesh is heir to, on revolt against the pleasures as well as the cares and sorrows of the world.

The first requisite of His teaching is thus a frank recognition of the facts of life, a just estimate of their values. The first essential is a realization that all conscious existence is enveloped in suffering! . . .

The maladies of the body are only too well-matched by the ills of the mind: striving and failure, frustrated ambition, mortified passion, baffled hope and disappointed endeavor, inexpressible bereavement, love wrecked by accident, disease or death. What anguish of mind there is in a single life-time, what grief and dejection, what lamentation and despair. . . .

This unescapable doom hangs over all felicity, frustrates all hope, poisons all joy. No one can escape it, whether deity, man or demon. The gods[16] in their celestial hostelries, however splendid they may be, and their life however glorious, some of them redoubtable tyrants, others compassionate protectors—they, too, are dominated by the same laws of decrepitude and dissolution as ours. How can they, deluded by their folly, save the world from suffering when they have not even freed themselves therefrom? . . .

That His was an unattractive doctrine the Buddha himself realised, and we are told that, for a brief moment after His Enlightenment, He wondered whether it would be worthwhile carrying such a message to men who were blinded by passion and wrapt in the darkness of ignorance. But then He recalled that it was for this that He laboured throughout countless lives; He knew that among men there were many whose minds were dulled by hardly any dust at all: they would understand. . . .[17]

2. The Doctrines of Karma and No-Self

Life is thus merely a phenomenon, or, rather, a series, a succession of phenomena, produced by the law of cause and effect. An individual existence is to be looked upon not as something permanent but as a succession of changes, as something that is always passing away. Each of us is merely a combination of material and mental qualities; every person or thing or god is thus a "putting together," a compound, what the Buddha calls a "sankhara." In each individual without exception the relation of the component, constituent parts is ever changing so that the compound is never the same for two consecutive moments. And this compound, this individual, remains separate as long as it persists in Samsara or existence as we know it. It is this separateness which is the cause of life and, therefore, of sorrow. I am I and you are you: if I am hungry and see you eat, I am not satisfied. If I have a toothache it is I who suffer, not you. That is because all our experiences are included in a single body. Hunger and pain are experiences that each separate self must endure; they can be removed when their cause, their ultimate cause, is removed and then the sense of separateness will also be automatically removed. Till such time the continuity of a person is maintained, through birth in this life and in many other lives. Our present life is only a link in the infinite chain of existence; what subsists is only the unbroken continuity of the processes that constitute life. . . .

As long as the cause of life persists, the sense of separateness, the craving for existence, so long will life continue; remove the cause of life and life does not come about. Remove the clinging to life and life is not continued. . . . It is kamma [i.e., karma], our actions, our thoughts and words, produced by this craving, that keeps the process going. Like the current of a river is life. A person standing on the bank thinks the river is the same though not a drop of water which he sees at any point remains where it was a moment ago. The beginning and end of the river are called source and mouth, though they are still composed of the same water as the rest of the river; even so are the source and mouth of the river of life called birth and death though still composed of the water of life. At death, the flow of the stream from life to life seems to be interrupted but there is no real interruption, only a more obvious, a more violent breach in the continuity than in normal life. To the Buddhist death is not anything very important but merely an incident between one life and its successor. Birth and death have great significance only to those who believe in a single life. . . .

If at death the craving for life has not been completely destroyed then this craving gathers fresh life, body and mind. The result is a new individual, new in a sense.. There is nothing that passes from one life to another. It is the kamma produced by us in our previous lives and in this life that brings about the new life. The new body and mind is [sic] merely the result of the previous body and mind. Just as this life is the result of the kamma of past lives so our next life is the product of that kamma plus the kamma of the present life. . . . The body and mind of the new life are not the same as the body and mind of the old, but only appropriate ones, i.e., those appropriate to the kamma that produces them. Somewhere in the various worlds—for this is only but one of many worlds—not necessarily spatially but conditionally, somewhere in the various worlds, our kamma finds precisely those conditions that are in tune for the rebirth.[18]

3. *Nirvana, the Transcendent State of Changelessness*

Nirvana is a state; as taught by the Buddha, it is the state which is the natural and inevitable result of the extinction of craving. It is the cessation of life as we know it; in a sense it is annihilation, but not the annihilation of self, for there is no self to annihilate. The fire has gone out because there is no more fuel to feed it. It is the annihilation of the illusion of self, of separateness. The whole of the clingings, affections for oneself, the desires, the appetites, the thirst, which surround or support this illusion, have all been destroyed, together with the evil, the ignorance, the hatred and greed and the lust which accompany it. They have died for lack of the nourishment that sustained them, never more to return. The heart has reached the final goal of all which, upon the ground of a perception of the true nature of things, has so completely loosed itself from everything that it no longer has any desires. Where there is no desire in the heart there is no attachment either. Where there is no attachment, there is also no sorrow. Where there is no sorrow, there is also no transiency, no change. And thus, with Nirvana, the true condition of eternal rest and birthless, changeless, deathless security is eternally attained. . . .

Because the Buddha sets out from the fact of sorrow in the shape of greed, hate and illusion, and so proceeds with the course of His thought, His system naturally eventuates in freedom from sorrow, the negation of greed, hate and illusion. Non-sorrow is the conclusion, it is the highest. By this transformation of sorrow into freedom from sorrow, nothing new is built up. It is a transition in our understanding, from an erroneous view into a correct one, and with that transition, even as transiency is transmuted into sorrow, so sorrow is transmuted into sorrowlessness. Nirvana is nothing but the destruction of an illusion that has its basis in me, and has arisen simultaneously with my arising. In our inmost depths this tremendous transmutation takes place, as it were, in a twinkling of our mind's eye. It comes in a flash of insight, of insight into the true nature of things. "Knowledge arose in me, the eye of truth flashed into me," says the Buddha, describing His experience as He won Enlightenment. The prisoner in Samsara, who is bound and chained by his own passions and desires for himself and his own presentation [sic; = preservation], whose prison walls were erected and sustained by himself, now finds that he is free; the fetters fall from him, the prison walls and roof and floor disappear. . . .

Nirvana implies nothing else but the clear, pure condition of freedom from sorrow, based upon freedom from desire, this in turn being founded upon the highest apprehension of the Truth about things, the realisation of that Truth. It is a condition which by itself is quite unexplainable, quite undefinable.[19]

4. *The Ultimately True, the Experience of Parinirvana*

When the saint—as he is called, the Arhant, the Perfect One —has attained Nirvana, he is not reborn anywhere for he is no longer subject to any of the laws that govern life and death. What exactly happens to him we cannot say, for all our thoughts, terms and modes of speech are bound up with the illusion of self and are, therefore, incapable of describing this state—which is called Parinirvana, the Final Release—which the Arhant attains after death, a state which is the very antithesis of life as known to us where there is no participation in any describable form of existence nor, indeed, of non-existence. It is an experience, not a speculation. All we can say about it is that it is beyond and outside all conditionings. Nothing can be said of that Beyond-the-world in the speech of this Within-the-world which will not in some way be false, misleading, untrue.

Parinirvana has been described as Nirvana freed of corporeality, Nirvana from which the body has dried up, withered away; sorrowlessness without an organ by which to become aware of itself, that is, the transition of sorrowlessness into timelessness, changelessness, perfect peace. Parinirvana is timeless, pure, uncoloured, unbesmirched of individuality. It stands to arising and passing away—to *Becoming*—not as *Being* but solely as *"No-more-Becoming."* Whether *"Not-Becoming"* resembles *"Being"* or whether it does not resemble it, who can know? The Buddha did not positively teach that this state involves the dissolution of conscious awareness as such, in its possibly universal as well as its obviously individual form. On the contrary the Buddha called the state *Amata*, the Deathless, Immortality. . . .

It is said that once the Buddha was definitely asked whether a Buddha, he who has attained Nirvana, exists or does not exist? The Buddha did not reply. . . .

It has been suggested that the Buddha's silence was due to the fact that the question was based on a false conception, that of the duality of Being and Not-Being. Had not the Buddha declared that "for him who knows according to the reality, there is neither Being, nor Not-Being"? Has He also not said that He repudiated the two opposing theories of annihilation and of the eternal life of the ego? All such theories are fabrications of our mind, dominated by error, illusion and wrong ideas that vitiate our reasoning. The Buddha neither exists nor ceases to exist after death, in the way in which our ignorance leads us to imagine those two states. Nor did He exist during what we call His *Life*, in the meaning which our ignorance gives to the world [sic; = word] "exist." It is the same with us, who do not "exist" in the way in which we imagine ourselves to exist, for "nothing is born, nothing dies," and all the theories of survival or annihilation which we evolve have their basis in the illusion of duality by which we are possessed; they are constructions of our fertile imagination.[20]

Whatever images and symbols are developed, Buddhism is always centered upon this reversal of transitoriness: changelessness, *Nirvana*. To the question, what is the ultimacy of changelessness?, Buddhism will give only the answer of the liberating mystical experience in which the very existence of changelessness is discovered. Language and concept as human and hence as phenomenal, and thus somehow illusory, can do no more than designate man's ultimacy by a negation: changelessness as a word, as the denial of transitoriness. The ineffability of this ultimacy is not thought of in terms of a relative limit to human knowing—human knowing in the order of phenomenal experience is simply irrelevant. Yet, of course, the human side of the paradox asserts itself in the Buddhist consciousness *to seek*, with its implied realization that its recognition of the meaninglessness and frustration in existence is not the end-product (as with most contemporary Western existentialists) but the statement of the problem to be solved and to which there certainly is a solution.

In the *Manual of the Heart of the Perfection of the Wisdom of the Other Shore* the meaning of the paradox is presented as the process of life symbolized by the passage over the sea from the shore of illusion and unknowing to the *Other Shore:*

> All the Enlightened Ones of the past, present and future,
> cleaving to the Wisdom of the Other Shore,
> have awakened to the highest, perfect, complete awakening.
> Therefore, one should know
> the Wisdom of the Other Shore
> is the great mystic formula,
> the mystic formula of great Wisdom,
> the most excellent mystic formula,
> the peerless mystic formula,
> capable of allaying every suffering.
> It is truth because it is not falsehood.
> A mystic formula has been given

in the Wisdom of the Other Shore.
It sounds as follows:

O you who are gone, who are gone,
who are gone to the Other Shore,
who have landed on the Other Shore:
O YOU ENLIGHTENMENT, HAIL! [21]

The Ultimacy proposed for man by religion is here not known
or knowable; the Wisdom of the Other Shore is the State of
Changelessness, Existence, which cannot be properly named. Its
experience radically transcends any other experience. Phenomenal experience is irrelevant to it, but it, as liberation, is not irrelevant to phenomenal experience! Hence, it is the Wisdom, not the
knowledge, of the Other Shore. Its Ultimacy is in *being awake,* not
in seeing or knowing *something*. And therefore *being awake* is absolutely relevant to further phenomenal experience. Zen Buddhism
has spoken of it: before Enlightenment one gazes at a tree and
the moon; one is Enlightened-Awakened, to No-Self, and there is
no-thing, no *this-that;* and *therefore* one sees a tree and the moon. It
is absurd to ask *what* element or factor constitutes the difference,
for the difference is in the actual experiential process not in any
thing. Thus, Ultimacy in the *theos*-category structure for Buddhism should be spoken of as Truth rather than as Being, or, better, as the Ultimate True (a contrast or coordination not at all
unknown in the West, especially in mystical literature).

As we shift our attention westward for further comparative
material the theological paradox of the content of the *theos*-cate-
gory is highlighted in an extraordinary manner because of the
dominance in most Western religious Traditions of proposed historic revelation made by Divinity to man. In the religious Traditions of Judaism, Zoroastrianism, Christianity and Islam we have
a common fundamental structure in the paradox of Divinity,
mysterious and unknowable, being revealed to mankind so that
man can respond to the reality of God with a new and significant
awareness.

"Divinity," "God" and related terms express in themselves the

difference in orientation between East and West, as just discussed. The West, with its usual first interest in individuation
and phenomenal analysis, structures religious experience in
terms of metaphysical relationship—ultimately subject/object—
rather than in terms of an experiencing-process. These two structures can imply each other (and perhaps they must imply each
other), but one or the other is the "way into" the religious experience in accord with the way in which sharing takes place and
consequently with the form of the ongoing historic tradition of
experiencing-sharing. The East, seeing Ultimacy in the structure
of man experiencing Oneness (or Changelessness, or Principle
and so on), necessarily must see *man moving, changing, awakening*.
The West, seeing Ultimacy in the structure man-and-God (or the
One, the Good, Being, and so on), necessarily must see *God moving
man*.

IV

For Zoroaster the cleavage between matter and spirit makes
impossible the reduction of Divinity to any image of man's phenomenal experience. The cult symbol of light or fire does not
show what God is like but points to the enlightenment man must
seek if he is to reach God. God reveals a pattern of life which
man must lead, a way of righteousness, so that man can survive
the Day of Judgment coming at the end of time—but man cannot truly know God until after the Judgment and his transformation when he as spirit is freed from matter. (Man as spirit-and-
matter is not thought of as part spirit and part matter, or a mixture of bits of each, something like mud as a mixture of particles
of earth with droplets of water, or in the later Greek sense of a
spirit encased in matter. Man has his origin in the fusion of matter and spirit which results in a being of a new sort, and it is this
which is to be transformed into spirit. And spirit-and-matter existence while derived from matter and spirit is a *tertium quid* until
transformed, and thus man as he is cannot be an image of God

except in terms of the final state of the righteous.) Thus, as man follows the revealed way of righteousness, God, the Wise Lord, remains a mystery yet is somehow manifested through the happenings of existence.

> O Wise Lord, I recognized you as the Holy One,
> When at the beginning, at the birth of life, I saw you
> Establish a recompense for deeds and words:
> Evil to the evil and good to the good,
> Through your Wisdom at the last crisis of creation.
>
> (*Gathas*, Yasna XLIII: 5)[22]

God is revealed, is recognized as the Holy One, insofar as man is transformed by knowing the Law of life, by knowing Judgment is coming, by giving worship appropriate to spirit, by following unquestioningly the dictates of Divine Will, by knowing the value of existence, by the renunciation of evil. (*Gathas*, Yasna XLIII: 5, 7, 9, 11, 13, 15)

For Judaism the entire significance of human history is bound up with the fact that God reveals Himself in an ongoing history of human fulfillment. God is the Lord-of-people, whose lives are bound up with Him through the Covenant whereby He has become their God and they have become His people. As a covenanted people their every act constitutes either a manifestation of the dominion of the Lord in this world or a rebellion whose punishment will further reveal God in history. God enlightens man with the Law, the "incarnation" of the Will of God, and simultaneously the living responsiveness of the people accepting it under the Covenant. The Law is the way of life which man is to live, and the awareness of this revelation is deepened by the actual historic process in which the Law is obeyed or not.

In every era of the development of Judaism the paradox of God as unknowable yet known in a tradition of revelation asserts itself. Israel at Sinai enters the Covenant, pledging observance of God's Will-Law as this is revealed, and God remains hidden and remote:

No man can see Me and live. (Exodus XXXIII:20)

As Israel is formed into a nation, God is totally present in every act of His elected people, yet there can be no image of Him, anything attempting a representation of Him must be cast aside. The succession of prophets bears constant witness to the intimacy of relationship between Israel and its Lord, proclaiming His Will in every event of importance, yet always insisting on the awe-inspiring remoteness of God from sinful man—the God whose ways cannot be known, who cannot be counselled, whose very Name must not be uttered.

We can catch something of the feeling of the community's experience of an historic moment of simultaneous intimacy and remoteness in the narration of the reaffirmation of the Covenant, as made under Ezra. This is the climactic event in the history of the formation of Israel from its beginnings and the re-formation following the Babylonian captivity, in which the earlier tradition emerges as Judaism (in the systematic sense). This process of forming and re-forming ever afterwards dominates Judaic thought, and properly, as Israel undergoes the tensions of the last two millennia to the present. The covenantal consciousness at the core of Judaism emerges fully in the Book of Nehemiah, as the summation of all the earlier development of experience and as the archetypal pattern for the future. The historic covenantal experience brings into one moment of consciousness the shared way of life of a people, the *logos*-category of known content, with the absoluteness of the Lord, the ineffable *theos*-category.

When the seventh month came, all the people gathered as one man on the square before the Water Gate. They asked Ezra the scribe to bring the Book of the Law of Moses which the Lord had prescribed for Israel. Accordingly, Ezra the priest brought the Law before the gathering, consisting of men, women and children old enough to understand. . . . From early morning until noon he read from the Book; all the people listened attentively to the Book of the Law.

Ezra opened the Book, and when he opened it all the people
stood up. Then Ezra blessed the Lord, the great God, and all the
people raised their hands and answered, "Amen! Amen!" Then
they bowed down and prostrated themselves face to the ground
before the Lord.

Each day from the first to the last Ezra read from the Book of the
Law of God, and they celebrated the feast for seven days. On the
eighth day as prescribed there was a solemn assembly. . . . They
stood confessing their sins and the transgressions of their ancestors.

As a result of all this we make a firm agreement in writing.

[All] the people . . . join with their kinsmen and leaders and
under curse and oath undertake to walk according to the Law of
God given through Moses, the servant of God, and to observe
and practice all the commandments of God our Lord, His customs and His Laws.

(Nehemiah, VIII; IX; X. passim)

Later, as the systematized analysis of formal theology is developed within Judaism, the mystery of God as totally unknowable
but revealed in His covenantal Law as His Will inevitably becomes a central area of inquiry. The paradox is also found in the
development of the several mystical traditions of Judaism. Here
we find patterns of expression and modes of approach somewhat
reminiscent of the mysticism of India and China. God cannot be
reached by human knowledge but somehow in a process of ultimate unification man can be enlightened, can achieve a wisdom
which is not human knowledge and in this wisdom be involved in
God as God is. The Kaballah, though so often reduced to the
crude abuses of divining and sorcery, expresses the mysterious
distinction between knowledge and wisdom in a striking manner.
And the effect of the Kaballah tradition on Jewish folklore, especially through Hasidism, testifies that this distinction as an attempt to express the theological paradox is one which can be
popularly grasped at least to some extent.

V

With roots deep in the prophetic tradition of Israel, the vitality of Islam is founded upon a dialectic of Divinity revealed dramatically in His own Words yet remaining completely mysterious. In the Qur'ān the Will of God for man is made manifest as Divine Compassion so that man will turn to God in the complete surrender of Faith, worshipping that which remains beyond him by a life of grateful and joyous submission to the Absolute.

The power of Qur'anic revelations arises from the positive Divine-human relationship established in the warm Compassion of God for man and man's responsiveness of filial love. The Qur'ān calls for faithfulness on the part of man because of the Absoluteness of God, yet this is never abstracted from the deeply personal situation of God and man together. The most prominent attribute of God in Muslim prayer and personal spirituality is *The Compassionate,* which identifies God to Muhammad in the opening of the revelation to him.

The acceptance of the Qur'ān as the ultimate manifestation of Divine Will leads Muslim thought inevitably to an elaboration of the dialectical tension in which the very words and language of the Qur'ān are sacred—are God's, not man's—and further, that the Qur'ān given to man, though complete and final as revelation, nonetheless is but a small portion of a Heavenly Qur'ān, the infinity of Divine Wisdom Itself. Through the historic Qur'ān, man can know who he really is, can know the meaning of creation and the world as it develops throughout time, can know his relationship to God and, most important of all, can know through his loving faithfulness what his own creatureliness actually is in the face of the Absoluteness of Divine Majesty. Islam effectively translates the fundamental theological paradox from an intellectual problem to the awareness of the everyday, moment-to-moment living out of the religious situation.

The Muslim prays in the words of the Qur'ān, hearing his own voice speak the Words of God. What happens to him each day, his success and his failure, are all the concrete realities of the Divine Will, and yet they are also always man's own realities. Destiny is not the fatalist absoluteness of what is decreed, but is the fulfillment of selfhood from deep within the individual, since the Will of The Compassionate is a calling to faithfulness rather than a deterministic imposition.

Thus, in the opening of revelation to the Prophet creation, (revealed) wisdom and faithfulness together form the situation of the religious experience:

> Read, in the Name of your Lord Who created,
> Who created man from congealed blood.
> Read, for your Lord is most generous,
> He Who taught by the Pen:
> He taught man what he did not know.
> Indeed man is rebellious
> for he deems himself not accountable (to Law)—
> But to your Lord is the Return.
>> (Qur'ān, XCVI: 1–8)

And faithfulness is deeply human, not abstract:

> Did you see the one who repudiates the Faith?
> It is he who maltreats the orphan
> and does not exhort (all) to feed the poor.
>> (Qur'ān, CVII)

The dynamics of the paradox have one of their most forceful expressions in the development of Sufist mysticism. Sufism recognizes in the Qur'ān both the manifestation of God and the call to approach the unknowable God through mystic union. Though God speaks in the Qur'ān to reveal His Will to man, the mystic also finds in the Qur'ān the *ayah*, or signs, of the interior mystery of the Presence of God. The Qur'ān not only reveals but it also contains hidden mystical meaning to be approached through contemplation.

Sufism identifies a number of passages as signs of the mystery:

Wherever you turn yourselves to pray, there is the Face of God.
>> (Q., II: 109)

Say: God! and leave them to their vain amusements. (Q., VI: 91)
They do not make a proper estimation of God. (Q., VI: 91)
God knows, but you do not know. (Q., III: 59)

The popular mystic devotion of the litany of the Ninety-Nine
Beautiful Names of God is another demonstration of the paradox. There are several traditional lists of Names and the limitation to ninety-nine is symbolic and not intended as a definitive
number. But all the variations share the same structure: a series
of names designating divine attributes, referring to God as Creator, Protector, King, Merciful, Generous, Strong, Glorious, Eternal, but subtly opposed to these attributive names is the One
Hundredth Name, *Allah*, called the Essential Name—the name
of revelation in the Qur'ān, the mysterious unexplained sound
which is the proper identification of Divinity. Thus, on the level
of popular mysticism the Ninety-Nine Names proclaim that God
is known, while the One Hundredth Name calls upon the be-
liever to surrender himself to the mystery of Faith.

VI

The place and function of the paradox within the Christian
Tradition have always been involved in a peculiar ambiguity.
Christianity, like Islam, has deep roots in the prophetic tradition
of Israel. From this source the recognition of God as unknowable
in Himself is therefore an element to be found in the earliest
documents. If anything, the Christian conviction concerning the
nature and manner of revelation should tend to heighten the importance of divine ineffability. For revelation as historic incarnation emphasizes God as unknowable in Himself, and known in
the sense of experienced insofar as one knows or experiences the
historic man who, as a man, is in total union with the Godhead.
Incarnational revelation thus is centered upon a medium, a
human being who is completely a human being and who always
remains such and yet is so united to Divinity that to experience
this man is to experience God fully.

Since Christianity affirms that this incarnational revelation is a historic reality, necessarily many historic events or elements must be accounted for implicitly or explicitly in anything approaching a full statement of the mystery of God revealed. But the core of Christian revelation is not to be identified with the events as such or with any particular teachings or understandings of man in his religious relationship, important as these are. Christianity, ultimately, is the recognition of the historic reality of Christ: who and what He actually is, and who and what man must be as a consequence. For the Christian, the issue of revelation in terms of the human situation is clear. If man seeks fulfillment, and if this fulfillment is not simply from within himself as he is, then the basis for the fulfillment as real must somehow "come into" the process of human existence.[23] If there is to be fulfillment it necessarily must be real for man as man is and hence it must be an actual historic fulfillment taking place in a human manner. In other words, human fulfillment in an Absolute must take place through a human. (And if this has not taken place through Jesus of Nazareth then it must take place through someone else, some real human being, if it is to take place at all.) Christianity sees itself as a historic religion not simply in the sense of being founded within a period of recorded chronological history but as historic in the ultimate meaning that man as he really is can have.

This Christian consciousness of revelation as theophany calls for a continuing dynamism in the affirmation that God as He is in Himself is always unknowable but in Christ is known through the *human* reality of Jesus. In the historic development of Christian thought, especially in the formal theological traditions, the full impact of the paradox tends to be lost, sometimes the paradox is simply ignored and the crucial balance in the insight of the primitive period is all but forgotten. And popular Christianity in almost all of its many forms has little or no awareness of this central ambiguity. In the context of certain contemporary theological developments and their popularization it is interesting to note how often an almost violent reaction occurs against the serious proposal of ineffability especially when there is the further proposal to carry the implications to their logical conclusions. With the present popular reemphasis on Scripture and the new attempts being made to develop a complete Scriptural theology, the serious assertion of the ineffability of God is even countered with the criticism that the assertion is not itself biblically based! There is no doubt that the strong statement of the paradox can be quite disturbing especially for a simplified theological approach, systematic or popular. Yet even a rather superficial acquaintance with Pauline or Johannine literature should be sufficient demonstration of a Scriptural basis for the problem as one which must be faced within the Christian Tradition.

The principal developments of systematized Christian theology have always expressed the paradox, however they have treated its implications. In the Eastern tradition the so-called negative theology of John Chrysostom takes up the paradox boldly and simply does not allow for an undercutting of ineffability by denying the possibility of any positive conceptualization of Divinity. Chrysostom's intellectual commitment has a profound influence on all future development of the Eastern tradition, even though the full impact of his so-called negativism is often somewhat obscured. Of the Eastern Fathers, Chrysostom is the most cited in the West, his negative theology is known, but for the most part Westerners tend to ignore what Chrysostom recognized.

Chrysostom opposed unequivocally those who maintained that knowledge of God was possible through conceptualization or comprehension: "He who seeks to apprehend His essential being insults God." [24] Further:

We call Him the inexpressible, the unthinkable God, the invisible, the inapprehensible; who quells the power of human speech and transcends the grasp of mortal thought; inaccessible to the angels, unbeheld of the Seraphim, unimagined of the Cherubim, invisible to principalities and authorities and powers, and, in a word, to all creation. [25]

Among the Greek Fathers Chrysostom is not at all alone in his insistence upon an apophatic theology. And so, for example, we find the concurrence of Gregory of Nyssa in the *Contra Eunomium:*

But if one asks for an interpretation or description or explanation of the divine nature we shall not deny that in such a science as this we are unlearned. . . . For there is no way of comprehending the indefinable as it is by a scheme of words. For the Divine is too noble and too lofty to be indicated by a name: and we have learned to honor by silence that which transcends reason and thought.[26]

If we look to Thomas Aquinas as the Western theologian most committed to the development of systematized thought prior to the Renaissance, we will find an enlightening but all too often ignored dimension of his insight. He is keenly aware of the intellectual problem raised by the assertion of ineffability. But he wishes to achieve a balance between this and the Western intellectual heritage of positive philosophical statement. Thus, rather than following the technique of negative expression characteristic of Chrysostom, Thomas uses positive expression but carefully establishes a proper negative norm for the evaluation of theological language.

In the opening sections of the *Summa Theologiae* Thomas sets forth several principles for the interpretation of the conceptual structure he will use in systematizing the Christian Tradition. He proposes these considerations as derived from reason and hence as providing a proper key for the meaningful use and understanding of language. Whatever one might think of the derivation of these principles philosophically, they provide us with a fairly clear understanding of his insight into the limits of religious knowledge.

Enunciated as a fundamental principle Thomas asserts without reservation that what God is is unknowable:

The Nature of God, however, cannot be seen by any created similitude (that is, concept) representing the Divine Nature itself *as it really is.*[27]

If he follows this principle rigorously, then the many concepts he advances concerning divine nature are simply positive statements used to express a negative theology. If a concept cannot represent the divine nature as it is then, logically, theological concepts of God are advanced to represent the divine nature *as it really is not!* —and hence actually to represent man related to God, the human and hence knowable dimension of religious knowledge. Some object to this interpretation of Thomas' principle as too rigorous, but other related texts from the early sections of the *Summa* carry forward its logical implications. Thus, Thomas identifies Divinity as existence, asserting that in God the Divine Nature is the Divine Existence.[28] To emphasize this assertion he makes explicit the absoluteness intended in the term *Divine Existence* with the statement, "God is not a being but being itself." [29] This is further extended by the meanings given to other possible attributions. Thus, not only is the Divine Nature the Divine Existence, but the Divine Intellect and the Divine Will are also completely identical in themselves with the Divine Existence. Hence Thomas has radically altered a previous pattern of Western language by reducing four vocabulary elements to one meaning: Existence, Nature, Intellect and Will mean *Existence.*[30]

If we proceed on the basis of these fundamental statements through the development of the *Summa,* the theological system will be observed to be completely consistent in elaborating the implications of its first principles. In terms of language and its use in interpretation in theology, Thomas attempted and achieved the development of a conceptually positive expression of a negative theology. For the theological historian, however, the general failure of Thomists to recognize this is perhaps more remarkable than the system itself. And so at the Reformation Period, for example, the later Catholic Scholastics became embroiled in the famous Grace Controversy, with two opposed factions explaining human election to Salvation as determined either by an act of the Divine Will or by an act of the Divine Intellect, apparently forgetting that Thomas' identification of Intellect and Will with Divine Existence reduced both positions to linguistic nonsense.

As a final example drawn from Western Christianity, the theological developments of the Reformation Period bring a new emphasis to the paradox as a central issue. Calvin's biblically oriented theology, to cite but one of the several major creative theologians of Protestant Christianity, places a strong emphasis on the recognition of God as completely mysterious and yet as revealed through his Word. When Calvin speaks of the Divinity as such it is always in terms of the Divine Majesty. This designation is the insistence on the Absoluteness of God, the transcendence with its infinite gulf separating man. For Calvin, we can speak only of the "infinite fullness of God." [31] In thus speaking we are not expressing knowledge of God but rather we "acknowledge that in the Lord alone are to be found true wisdom, solid strength, perfect goodness and unspotted righteousness." [32] The reflection of the Divine Majesty is to be found throughout the universe in that all things as creatures bear the imprint of the Creator. However, knowledge of God through creatures does not reveal what God is in Himself, but reveals the relationship of total subjection of creature to Creator. This is, again, an acknowledgment rather than knowledge.

Yet this is not even possible for man as he is due to the depravity of man's fallen nature. The revelation of God in Christ as Redeemer enables man to acknowledge the relationship of creature to Creator and, of course, further enlightens man as to God's Will for him and the way of life for the elect. For our purposes the important point to note is the prominence given to the assertion of God as unknowable. This particular approach has insured only a formal theological place for the paradox but, generally, not a popular awareness on the level of individual religious consciousness.

VII

All of this material has been drawn from religious traditions with a written literature and which can be expected to be able to participate actively in the process of convergence which concerns us. Although what are usually classed as primitive religions could be passed over both because it is difficult to evaluate their material (even more so than any comparative study of the advanced traditions!) and because they are at least unlikely participants in convergence, it is interesting to be able to observe the rather regular recurrence in them of this same problem of ineffability. Many of the myth-symbols betray this by their incompleteness or patterns of internal self-contradiction (which cannot be ascribed to mental inferiority, so often presumed in colonialist contact with "the natives"). Even more important are the relatively clear religious structures involving some god or being who is "unknown," or who "stands behind" the knowable deities, a shadowy Presence "before creation," and so on.

One example of interest, drawn from pre-Columbian Aztec religion, will illustrate this pattern and possibly serve as an indication that the later "speculative" or "theological" concern with the ineffable on the part of advanced traditions is not discontinuous with the formation of primitive myth-symbol traditions. (In one respect especially the Aztecs are ideal for our present purpose since they stand developmentally somewhere between a traditional tribal culture and complex advanced civilization, and are completely independent of either East or West.)

Beyond all the complex of divinities representative of nature and the agricultural cycle, and dominating the intricate astronomical calendar with its personified mathematical deities, the Aztecs revered a remote being, Ometecuhtli, or the Two-fold Lord. The name indicates an affirmation of unity in difference, anthropomorphically of male and female forces. Ometecuhtli exists outside of space and time and is the source of all existence including that of the "gods." He is symbolized by the Pole Star, the apparently unmoving center of the celestial cosmos. He is the source of every-day life, nourishment and fire. He is often depicted with a temple in flames to indicate his complete independence of space-time temples, sacrifices and ceremonies. Existence is so bound up with him that no spot on earth could be set aside as his place of worship since he is equally everywhere; so also with festal times since all lifetime and history is within him (and in the sacred calendar he therefore stands at the first day, *Ce Ci-pactli*, with the symbolism of the alligator as the Mother Earth and of the creator or fashioner deity Tonacatecuhtli, and this first day is the memorial of the original first day of creation). He is also the source of man's emotional and intellectual life, the greatest of his gifts without which existence would be a meaningless determinism. With all of the elaborate symbolism and deference expressing man's ultimate dependence upon him, the Twofold Lord remains for the Aztecs totally mysterious, and hence they serve the vast numbers of "gods" whom they *know*. They seek contact with him only at birth and death when all opposites resolve into his unity, when the whole cosmos could be seen as but a drop of water in his hand.

THE
FORMULATION
OF
THEOLOGY

I

The review of some of the major areas of man's religious development has taken up only one issue in a highly simplified (but, hopefully, not oversimplified) manner. Although this issue is of great importance in the consideration of several fundamental questions facing the study of religion today (and certainly that of convergence), the purpose of the review in the present context of theology is to delineate a crucial area of data which must be taken into account in any attempt to formulate a meaningful definition of theology and an understanding of the function of theology in the overall process of knowing. Hence this review is not designed to "prove" anything, but it does lay the groundwork for a structuring of theology which can hope to overarch the boundaries separating most systems of theology and religious traditions.

Working solely from what we can observe in the continuing paradoxical treatment of the *theos*-category on the part of actual systems, we must come to the following conclusions, subjectively

108

independent of the various separate traditions in which we as individuals stand.

First, the variety in the conceptualizations proposed comes from a wide range of factors in the individual tradition. Although the concepts proposed are proposed *because of religious experience,* the particular characteristics of the concepts do not derive from the experience itself (inevitably described as mysterious in the radical sense) but from the context in which the experience occurs, the context which necessarily embraces the entire range of our consciousness. Thus the actual conceptual content being proposed is not valid simply because the religious experience is valid. The variety in theological expression must be accounted for by the range of materials which go to form the consciousness of the individuals who become involved in what they identify as unknowable. Theological content must pass the same judgment which we make in all the areas of our consciousness: how realistically does it express a human relationship which is real, which occurs in a real context and which must be really communicable if it is to be thought of as meaningful?

The second conclusion is intimately related to the first, namely, that the validity of the religious experience and hence of the recognition of mystery, ineffability, does not depend upon the way in which it is conceived. If the religious experience occurs, it occurs whether or not we have any way of accounting for it afterwards. If it is an actual experience then we can attempt to understand it or explain it but this can never "explain it away." Thus, if we say that the religious experience is expressive of one or another psychic need, this might well give some understanding of the context of its occurrence but it cannot deny the occurrence as such. Ultimately the question comes down to one facing all scientific inquiries: human experience of something takes place, the data to be studied; observable characteristics of the experience are analyzed and we attempt to establish relationships with other areas of our experience; but the conceptual representation of the experience and the formulated relationships are not the experience. Put another way, a theory advanced to provide an understanding of observed experience cannot be valid if it first calls for the denial of the data supposedly being studied.

As we have been observing, what we refer to as the *theos*-category in any attempted conceptualization reveals upon close analysis that there is no conceptual content as such as the "object" of the experience. Hence a theory which attempts to state what the "object" in the experience is cannot be addressing the religious experience as it actually occurs. Thus, for example, to propose that what people call the religious experience is actually a deep recognition of social cohesion attempts to substitute social cohesion—some *thing* which *is known*—for the "object" which *as actually experienced* is and remains in itself *unknown*, whatever type of conceptual content is proposed for the *theos*-category theologically. To accept a theory with an actual content for the "object" is to explain away or do away with the religious experience which, whatever it is, simply does not have a content-object.

(Perhaps passing mention should be made at this point of the possible relationship between that form of religious experience designated specifically as the mystical experience and the type of experience occurring through the use of halucinogenic drugs or their equivalent. The literature of traditional mysticism reveals two classes of materials in the reports of religious mystics: an extraordinary mass of variegated and emotionally-charged symbols, unusual sense-experiences and the like, and the affirmation that "behind" or "beyond" or "at the base of " all these is a contentless experience to which all the rest is subsequent subjective reaction. As reported the experience induced by drugs or fasting is not psychologically contentless, and thus whatever its relation within the experiencer, it cannot be simply equated with the experience which demands and allows only the identification *ineffability*.)[1]

Therefore we must make an adequate distinction between the problem of conceptualization and the inner experiential factor *which together* form the paradox of the *theos*-category. And as in the case of every paradox both components must be adequately maintained in the same context of their occurrence, lest we do the impossible and resolve the paradox!

There is a third and most important conclusion drawn from the first two taken together. Theology as a process of knowledge dealing with the religious experience in the context of an identifiable tradition does not deal with the *theos*-category directly but only relationally. That is, because of a particular kind of human experience a complex of relationships arises and is conceptualized within an actual historic setting. But our observation shows us that that toward which the relationship is oriented is unknown—unknowable—in terms of the actual knowing process, and hence a theological system as a system of knowing does not actually take account of the terminus of the orientation. Implicit in this recognition is the judgment that theology cannot even deal with the religious relationship as terminating in an object, an entity, an item of any sort. If it were to do so then we would be faced with a clear contradiction rendering all theological language nonsense, namely, in asserting that that which the *theos*-category stands for is genuinely unknowable there would have to be the simultaneously contradictory assertion that it is nonetheless known to be an object in a human subject-object relationship or an entity, whatever the kind, or an item among items. The assertion *ineffability* admits of no degrees.

Theology deals with a human subject in a particular kind of relationship. Because the human is in a line of experience we identify as religious he relates himself in a particular way to everyone and everything else. The consciousness of the religious experience terminates in the affirmation of *unknowing,* but this must not be violated by transforming the termination of the *consciousness* into an object corresponding to a subject.

Perhaps it is in this consideration that the real significance of the so-called negative theology can be seen when it insists on the assertion of the Sacred and refuses all conceptualizations. Here also we can see something of the proper impact intended by Aquinas in the statement "God is not a being but being itself."

If we accept the logic which insists that the *theos*-category does not represent an object of any sort, then what is it for theology, what is it that specifies theology as a discipline? According to what has been developed above, the *theos*-category is expressive of a particular kind of relationship of which man is conscious and which he attempts to conceptualize. The universal effect of the experience upon man is that he sees himself in a particular kind of relationship with other men and his world. He specifies this relationship in two ways. On the one hand he relates the content of his entire life to whatever ultimate significance the experience of the Sacred may have. On the other hand in the mysteriousness of the Sacred he perceives that the religious relationship is somehow *definitive*—definitive in the impact of what the Sacred is upon his consciousness and definitive in contrast to all other relationships. Both dimensions of definitiveness are rooted in the same experience but concentration upon that which reflects the Sacred in consciousness leads to mysticism while concentration upon that which expresses the correlation of human relationships leads to theology. The former calls for the continuing and vital assertion of ineffability in religion, while the latter allows man to attempt to relate the significance of religion as experiential to everything else in his life, hopefully to find a meaning for each area of relationship and an overarching meaning for the entire process of existence.

As an intellectual undertaking this differs necessarily from any other type of study of religion—historical, empirical or philosophical—in one all-important respect: theologizing is a creative process taking place within an actual tradition (or traditions) of *religious experiencing*. The theologizer is an experiencer, not simply a reporter, analyzer or theorizer, and hence he expects to contribute to the ongoing formation of the tradition of his own commitment. The creativity of the theologian does not inject an arbitrary or erratic factor into theologizing (and hence exclude theology from consideration as a possible scientific discipline); it is itself an integral part of the religious process which the theologian seeks to relate to all of experience. The creativity called for can be easily misinterpreted by members of the theologian's religious tradition who might expect that his role as a systematizer should exclude innovation—and hence a common Christian accusation against the medieval theologians for interpreting the Scriptural and Patristic Tradition in terms of philosophic systems and thereby innovating new lines of intellectual interest and development not at all contained within the traditions. Yet the integration achieved—created—by such a one as Aquinas could make it impossible to judge what specifically is Thomist *philosophy* and what specifically is Thomist *theology:* where is the line of demarkation between Thomas and Aristotle? where does Thomas modify Aristotle and where does Aristotle modify Thomas? With all their shortcomings perhaps the medieval theologians (Christian, Judaic and Muslim) are the most consistent exemplars of the tension implicit in the intellectual structure of theology: they seek to systematize the traditions of religious experience through the discipline of intellectual instruments (in their case the Platonic and Aristotelian philosophical systems), and as experiencers create new dimensions within their traditions as the process of systematization itself reveals unexpected relationships.

At this point it is at last possible to offer a definition of theology, proposed as a general definition of theology as a knowing process (and thus any one theological tradition would require particular specification of historic context if this definition is to be applied meaningfully). Within the limits set by the orientation developed here, theology may be defined as *the systematization of man's experience of definitive relationship.*

Systematization presumes that the theological enterprise is basically intellectual. It is concerned with man as religious but it is not itself a religious act. As a specified area in the knowing process it must reflect adequately the characteristics appropriate to knowledge. Rigorously pursued, this should itself guarantee the continuity of theology with the other branches of knowledge, a continuity often sacrificed or ignored in the past and whose restoration has become such a contemporary preoccupation.

It is the systematization of man's experience, and therefore it must deal with man as he actually is (and this must include the theologizer as he actually is). Thus the struggle to establish our full recognition of man as individual and social, and the realization that these two dimensions constitute a dynamic complementarity rather than a tension threatening one or the other are issues proper to theology itself. Theology must reflect the ongoing character of man's experience and not be caught in the error of presuming that experience from the past can be transmitted adequately to the present or future. Theology must deal with the perplexing fact that meaningful continuity is possible since the understanding of experience is communicable, yet change must occur in the very communication and further experience precludes any closed system.

In the systematization of man's experience of definitive relationship theology at all times must deal with the fundamental paradox so often stressed here, by limiting its attempts to systematize to the observable relationship which actually occurs in men. It is the definitiveness of this relationship as contrasted with the relativity of all others which guarantees that theology will remain oriented toward the full reality at the root of the experience, even though it is inconceivable. Focused upon the definitiveness of the relationship, theology will also remain in communication with the rest of knowledge built around the attempt to articulate man's meaning.

Specific theological systems, since they reflect the religious traditions which give rise to them, embody the particular characteristics of these traditions as well as reflect a wide range of factors operative within the socio-cultural context. Religious traditions heavily dependent upon historic personages and events will necessarily be represented by theological systems which emphasize concepts relating the definitiveness of the relationship as concretely experienced. Traditions centered upon symbol and myth involvement will develop theological systematization appropriately ignoring narrative history. The specific characteristics of each theological system will be understood properly only in terms of the total religious tradition in which it arises. Regardless of conceptualization, however, we will observe as a basic unitive factor among them all the insistence that man recognize that there is a type of relationship in his life which overrides all others, which represents ultimate values and which somehow embodies his own real significance and that of everything else, and thus is ineffably "other."

II

If our concern for the nature and function of theology calls for a traditional evaluation of theology as a science, we must insist on a formulation which is continuous with the other varieties of knowing designated sciences. Although this might seem obvious, at least in the West we have witnessed a long and meaningless struggle between theologians and scientists accidentally but effectively cut off from one another. Theologians too often have insisted that theology is some sort of super-science overriding the other, "lower" sciences and that theology is called to sit in judgment upon their findings and very principles. Conceived of as the *science of God*, the scientist has been called upon to submit to a higher authority of theological judgment in virtually every apparent conflict. On the other side, scientists have all too often lost sight of the fact that science is not an abstraction and cannot be hypostasized, but must always be recognized as the on-going process of human knowing. As such science must be seen as continuous with all other aspects of knowing, including the systematized attempt to know something of the significance of religious experience in both the individual occurrence and the continuing and elaborated occurrence of historic social religion.

Only insofar as theology is recognized as a systematization of human experience can it be thought of as a science among the other sciences. There is no other basis for the scientific character of theology (even for those who would insist that theology must be the "queen of sciences"). The continuity of theology with the other sciences is not to be *achieved* or *restored*, it is simply a self-demonstrated fact if it shares the disciplinary characteristics which constitute any branch of learning as a science. On this issue a comparison of apparent extremes will provide sufficient demonstration. Are theology and physics sciences together? Although he does not address himself to this question, the renowned physicist Niels Bohr in the introductory essay in *Atomic Theory and the Description of Nature* clearly stands in the affirmative if the fundamental structure of theology is a systematization of human experience.

He says, first of all:

The task of science is both to extend the range of our experience and to reduce it to order. . . . Only by experience itself do we come to recognize those laws which grant us a comprehensive view of the diversity of phenomena. As our knowledge becomes wider, we must always be prepared, therefore, to expect alterations in the points of view best suited to the ordering of our experience. . . . All new experience makes its appearance within the frame of our customary points of view and forms of perception.[2]

Science, thus, is both an ordering and extension of experience. Investigation of the experience results in a recognition of patterns allowing us to erect a structure, theory and law. However this itself extends the pattern of experience and hence new experience occurs within the framework developed for previous experience, and this in turn brings about changes in that framework.

This process occurs in physics and clearly is the same process occurring in theology: individual religious experience and the complex traditions of such experience with their full historic contexts are brought into order and theory and law are formulated— and always within the thrust of the on-going human historical situation.

Next, Bohr states:

. . . . We are concerned with expedients which enable us to express in a consistent manner essential aspects of the phenomena.[3]

Theological systems, as is the case with physics, have taken up a variety of instruments ("expedients") in the attempt to give meaningful expression to the happenings which constitute a religious tradition. In fact, the schools of theology (or the equivalents) of all traditions are identified primarily by the type of expedient which they employ, such as the intellectual structures of philosophical systems, structures drawn from evaluations of sacred writings proper to the religious tradition, and so forth. In other words, theological systems develop around the use of *models* employed to elaborate analogies which interconnect a wide variety of experience, in much the same way that physics uses models drawn from mathematics.

Finally, Bohr adverts to the crucial problem of expression which occurs for physics in the discovery that subject and object cannot be distinguished unambiguously:

The impossibility of distinguishing in our customary way between physical phenomena and their observation places us, indeed, in a position quite similar to that which is so familiar in psychology where we are continually reminded of the *difficulty of distinguishing between subject and object*. It may perhaps appear at first sight that such an attitude towards physics would leave room for a mysticism which is contrary to the spirit of natural science. However, we can no more hope to attain to a clear understanding in physics without facing the difficulties arising in the shaping of concepts and in the use of the medium of expression than we can in other fields of human inquiry.[4]

For theology the comparable problem is the one we have viewed at some length: the meaningfulness of proposing conceptual content for the *theos*-category while experientially negating the category as knowable.

Whatever other issues may be raised by formulating theology directly in terms of human experience (in which the human can be studied in the individual and social contexts with all their ramifications, and the relationship experienced as definitive can also be studied within the context of concrete traditions, while an object as such corresponding to the human subject cannot be studied), such a formulation of theology demonstrably establishes it as a science in the same sense that other fields of knowledge are so categorized; yet it also establishes the basis for both its distinctive disciplinary requirements and its natural autonomy. Theology, thus constituted continuous with the other sciences, needs no defense for existence and needs no reconciliation. With regard to the process of the continuing convergence of knowledge, the only problem remaining for theology as such is the development of a consciousness on the part of theologians and other scientists of the *fact* of continuity, overcoming the all too understandable prejudices of the past.

Apart from the dialectical potential of binary mathematical models for theology, the concept of model in theory formation presumes multiplicity. Since the model is not the *thing,* it may be possible (or, more likely, it is probable) that more than one model is appropriate. This plurality of models may be structured either as alternates or as simultaneously complementary elements, each saying something else within the theory statement— but not successively or as part of a greater whole. A plurality of models need not indicate competition, calling for a choice as to the "better." It also does not indicate that it is simply not possible pragmatically to discern which is the "better." Each of the many models is saying something different at the same time, and the fact that this takes place has its own significance.

It might be useful to draw into this context some very insightful operative notions of the Nineteenth Century liberal theologian Horace Bushnell (1802–1876). While not looking beyond the implications of his commitment as a Christian, Bushnell in many ways is representative of the early explorations of a theology derived from experience rather than from extrinsic doctrinal orthodoxy. He strongly insists that theological systems take seriously the fact of ineffability; he reflects much of the first impact of the new science on theology, especially in the theological significance of man in the light of organic evolution and the immanence of Ultimacy in the historic process. While not at all con-

cerned with model concepts, and remaining within the framework of Christian theological systems, he nonetheless perceives
what a plurality of theological statements can mean:

A very great share of our theological questions, or disputes, originate in the incapacity of the parties to separate truths from their
forms, or to see how the same essential truth may clothe itself
under forms that are repugnant. . . . Since words are given, not
to imprison souls, but to express them, the variations continually
indulged by others are sure to render him as miserable in his anx-
ieties, as he is meagre in his contents, and busy in his quarrels.[5]

. . . . Accordingly we never come so near to a truly well rounded
view of any truth, as when it is offered paradoxically; that is,
under contradictions; that is, under two or more dictions, which,
taken as dictions, are contrary one to the other.[6]

Then, speaking concretely of the variety within the foundational materials of the Christian Tradition, he continues:

. . . . And then what shall we do?—what, for example, with the
trinity, the atonement, the bondage and freedom of sin? Shall we
say . . . this is all a medley of contradiction—mere nonsense, fit
only to be rejected? Shall we take up these bold antagonisms, as
many orthodox believers have done, seize upon some one symbol
as the real form of the truth, and compel all others to submit to
it; making, thus, as many sects as there are symbols, and as many
petty wars about each truth as it has sides or inches of surface?
Or shall we endeavor, with the Unitarians, to decoct the whole
mass of symbol, and draw off the extract into pitchers of our own;
fine, consistent, nicely-rounded pitchers, which, so far from setting out any where towards infinity, we can carry at pleasure by
the handle, and definitely measure by the eye?[7]

Rejecting these possibilities, each in its own way divisive (divisive of the religious community and of the process of continuity),
he proposes a unitive pluralism in which differences are embraced as complementary:

How, then, are we to receive it and come into its truth? Only in
the comprehensive manner just now suggested; not by destroying

the repugnances, but by allowing them to stand, offering our mind to their impressions, and allowing it to gravitate inwardly, towards that whole of truth, in which they coalesce. And when we are in that whole, we shall have no dozen propositions of our own in which to give it forth; neither will it be a whole which we can set before the world, standing on one leg, in a perfectly definite shape, clear of all mystery: but it will be such a whole as requires a whole universe of rite, symbol, incarnation, historic breathings, and poetic fires, to give it expression,—in a word, just what it now has.[8]

Bushnell is developing these considerations not, of course, in terms of empirical models, but from within the actual process of religious experience. His context is Christianity with a specific concern for the genetic materials of the Scriptures. His experience within that context tells him he must integrate what he refers to as *truth* with its concreteness of *expression*. We can speak of religious experience and religious tradition as if they were divisible in actuality. We can speak of *truth* as if it were totally abstracted from its *expression*. If we do, the intellectual (theological) task within religion would seem to be to find *the* expression which concretely fits *this* truth. But the fact is that whatever Ultimacy is in what we term religious experience, the *experiencing* is always concrete—within the on-going context of all the rest of our experiencing, intimately at one in all of our symbolization. Hence in the dialectic between *truth* and *expression*—*theos-* and *logos*-categories—we must expect multiplicity and diversity of expression insofar as the totality of the concreteness of our experiencing is multiple and diverse. And this expectation should not be seen as something pertaining only to the intellect. If the experience of Ultimacy really takes place, the experiencer knows this Ultimacy to be of actually universal significance—he must expect that the whole process of experiencing everything is integral to this significance, and hence that all the multiplicity and diversity of that process is proper to religious experiencing-expressing.

As we can see in the concrete instance of Bushnell's statements, unitive pluralism is something positively coherent. There is something about the actual process of religious experiencing which constitutes a norm whereby he rejects some attempted expressions (the variety is a medley of contradiction, or, one symbol only is the real form of truth, or, the decoction of the mass into one new form). This "something" is clearly part of the religious experiencing-expressing process itself, and not a norm standing outside the process. Positively, from within the process, the experiencer-expresser finds a responsiveness in the many diverse and complementing forms: his acceptance of these and rejection of the others is the same act of consciousness of *what is happening.*

Turning to the formation of theological systems, Bushnell notes:

. . . . Can there be produced, in human language, a complete and proper Christian theology; can the Christian truth be offered in the molds of any dogmatic statement? What is the Christian truth? Pre-eminently and principally, it is the expression of God. . . . The [theological] endeavor is, by means of expression, and under the laws of expression, to set forth God. . . . Well, if it be something for a poet to express man, it is doubtless somewhat more for a book to be constructed that will express God, and open His eternity to man. . . . Let me freely confess that, when I see the human teacher elaborating a phrase of speech, or mere dialectic proposition, that is going to tell what God could only show me by the history of ages. . . . I should be deeply shocked by his irreverence, if I were not rather occupied with pity for his infirmity.[9]

And:

. . . . [Theological propositions or systems] only give us the seeing of the authors, at the precise stand-point occupied by them, at the time, and they are true only as seen from that point. . . . Passing on, descending the current of time . . . we are brought to a different point. . . . It is not that the truth changes, but that we change. . . . It may even be necessary to change the forms, to hold us in the same truths. . . . Considering the infirmities of language, therefore, all formulas of doctrine should be held in a certain spirit of accommodation. They cannot be pressed to the letter, for the very sufficient reason that the letter is never true. They can be regarded as only proximate representations, and should therefore be accepted not as laws over belief, or opinion, but more as badges of consent and good understanding.[10]

III

Although he strives to make his point strongly, Bushnell's insistence on a tension between the reality of the religious experience and the relativity of its expression—not an external but an internal tension since experience and expression are integral—is revolutionary only insofar as theologians have so often fallen into the trap of equating the two factors as identical. Such oversimplification is attacked time and again in theological systems. We can recall, for example, the distinction made by Thomas Aquinas between thought-and-thing:

. . . . Truth is the correspondence between thought and thing. . . .[11] Properly speaking, truth resides only in the intellect. . . . Hence the mutability of truth must be regarded from the point of view of the intellect, whose truth consists in its conformity to the things understood.[12]

—which leads logically to a recognition of relativity in all theological communication. The relativity is rooted in the expression of experience, but must involve the experience as well insofar as the two are integral to each other. Following Aquinas' definition of truth as the correspondence or equation between thought and thing, is the thought ever identical with the thing? If the expression of the experience of Ultimacy is not the ultimate expression, can the experience be the ultimate experience? As with the previous consideration of the tension between the absolute ineffability of what the *theos*-category points to and the conceptual content proposed for the category, thought-and-thing or experiencing-expressing relativity is proper to the one who experiences. It is not the subjectivism of not knowing.

This tension between reality and word finds powerful expression in the text of the Qur'ān:

> God speaks to no man [i.e., does not *speak words*],
> except through inspiration or from behind the veil,
> or He may send a messenger who speaks through
> inspiration. . . .
> Even so We have inspired you [Muhammad]
> with a spirit of Our Command. (Qur'ān, XLII: 51–2)

Commenting on the significance of this passage, Fazlur Rahman notes that early Muslim theology "lacked the intellectual capacity to say both that the Qur'ān is entirely the Word of God and, in an ordinary sense, also entirely the word of Muhammad. The Qur'ān obviously holds both, for if it insists that it has come to the 'heart' of the Prophet, how can it be external to him? . . . But [theological] orthodoxy . . . made the Revelation of the Prophet entirely through the ear and external to him. . . . The modern Western picture of the Prophetic Revelation rests largely on this orthodox formulation rather than on the Qur'ān, as does, of course, the belief of the common Muslim." [13]

Examples from Judaism, Christianity and Islam—both from sacred texts and theological formulations—could be multiplied endlessly. The extended citations from Bushnell given above are designed to point up the problem raised by the recognition of theological relativity. Even though theologians and sacred texts themselves insist on it, nonetheless this relativity is ignored or positively subverted (such as by any form of fundamentalism)—and the reason is rooted in an inability to *guarantee* that relativity in theological formulation will not necessarily result in relativism in religious reality. Thus, as we read Bushnell (or Aquinas or Rahman) we can recognize the logic of their distinction but fail to find any *objective* instrument to allow the distinction to be functional. We seem to have but two choices: accept a radical application of relativity and allow each separate formulation to stand as valid in itself, ignoring the competing implications of other equally accepted formulations; or, accept only one formulation as valid, rejecting all variants. Put simply, it would appear that we must be either indifferentists or fundamentalists, whatever the proposed basis of our choice. But we can find in Bushnell a hint at another solution: "all formulas of doctrine should be held in a certain spirit of accommodation . . . regarded only as proximate representations. . . ." [14] (And this should remind us of Bohr's "expedients which enable us to express in a consistent manner essential aspects of the phenomena.") The limitations of Bushnell's proposal reveal another dimension of the importance of a contemporary mathematical model for theology.

In speaking before of the *theos-* and *logos-*category dialectic in terms of a binary model, we recognized in passing that this dialectical relationship could be multiplied internally for each category. Thus, for *logos-*category we have an integral dialectic between individuality and sociality; for *theos-*category we have an integral dialectic between the conceptual content given and the Ultimacy toward which the category points. Both dialectics presume multiplicity. Individuality and sociality cannot be confined to one form each—whatever the limits to the range of possibilities, multiple varieties do actually exist among the individuals and the social constellations of individuals who participate in religious relationship and who therefore inevitably bring their multiplicity into any realistic formulation of meaning for that relationship. Hence also inevitably the conceptual content of the *theos-*category must reflect this multiplicity if it is to be realistic. And, this is the point of greatest importance, this must be a *simultaneous multiplicity*. The complexity of the *logos-*category is a simultaneous complexity and so must effect the dynamics of the *theos-*category correspondingly.

And it is here that empirical models can be of great significance for a theology which must be pluralistic as well as unitive. For the contemporary development of empirical disciplines has been characterized by the recognition of the validity of theory statements not in terms of mutual exclusion but as a multiplicity of complementarities. To draw a (much simplified) example from physics, in the development of theory concerning subatomic divisions of matter, two categories, *particles* and *states* of matter, had been defined mathematically in terms of time. Particles were conceived of as characterized by a certain minimal time, beyond which matter was to be conceived of in terms of states; advance, however, narrowed the gap between particle and state to the point of non-distinction, and hence the problem: which theory structure should be used in any one instance, a statement of particle or of state? But if a choice is not made and both concepts are used simultaneously, two ways of speaking (each from a different vantage point and so with different relational knowledge) occur whose apparent "conflicts" themselves are the sources of new insights (including the possible insight that the whole line of theory leading to that point is not significant!). Such an example has empirical parallels elsewhere, for example in biology—as in the continuum in the evolutionary life-process with the "overlap" of the most extremely complex molecules and the most rudimentary apparent life-forms.

Not making an either-or choice, but a both-and, opens up for exploration otherwise unsuspected implications, insofar as the knowing process is recognized as open, and such openness as essential, not accidental.

Complementarity in a multiplicity of theological formulations arises necessarily from the dialectical nature of the dual category structure with each category itself multiple. This complementarity positively excludes either indifferentism or fundamentalism, since the inherent complexity must be maintained simultaneously. But as theological systematization is always dependent upon an actual and on-going historic process of integral experiencing-expressing, the systematizing of the expressions of a tradition is necessarily held within a specific range of meaning. What is within this range cannot be pre-defined since we are dealing with a dynamic process. But at any one point the experiencers inevitably judge any expression as to whether or not there is correspondence with their experience at that moment. And they can expect change for the future consonant with the process of change in the past of the continuum, and so expect new expressions. To answer the question, how do they *know* what does or does not correspond?, we would have to be able to resolve the internal tension within the *theos*-category between content and the Ultimacy for which the content is proposed. We must be content to observe that participants in religious traditions regularly make such judgments and feel the imperative to do so.

The complementarity of simultaneous multiplicity, therefore, is a necessary and objective instrument of theology insofar as the complexity of the religious process is recognized and theologizing remains integral to it. Complementarity is the key to any attempt to extend the range of any one religious tradition to meet and integrate with another. Only this instrument is able to accept the authenticity of diversity and allow the production of new meaning within each of the significance of the integration. As seen through complementarity, religious pluralism ceases to be divisive and becomes the paradoxical basis of a new unity.

The dynamics of the *logos*-category occurs in the relationship of man as an individual to man as social, the basis for the singularity of the religious experience as it actually occurs within any one person and the unity of the effects of such singular experience in the development of the religious tradition in which many individuals participate as socially united, communicating and evolving the meaning of the experience. Within the *theos*-category there is a dialectical relationship between the proposition of concrete conceptual content and the experiential recognition that that which this category embraces is unknowable—dynamically allowing and calling for a wide range of meaning, ultimately the basis for religious communication and convergence on any level, including the universal convergence toward which we now seem to be drawn.

THE
HISTORIC
THEOLOGICAL
TRADITIONS

I

Before taking up an exploration of the potential complementarity of religious traditions in convergence, it is necessary to make explicit the extension of theology as a form of discipline beyond its previous limitation within Judaism, Christianity and Islam. Such an extension has been implied in many of our considerations up to this point, and sooner or later we are required to judge the validity of whether or not it is proper to propose theologizing for non-Western Traditions (and perhaps also whether or not it is really necessary).

The definition for theology just developed certainly allows for the application of theological discipline to the materials of any tradition. But before we conclude too quickly that therefore theology can be proper to the non-Western Traditions we must evaluate the definition in the light of the historic theological developments of the Western Traditions themselves. To put it bluntly, does this definition of theology fit the historic Western concept of

127

theology? Following the best tradition of the practicing theologians, we can answer both yes and no!

The major attempt of the present undertaking is to develop a new formulation of what theology is or is to be within the context of a radically new religious situation. Quite appropriately the understanding of theology heretofore has been framed according to different interests. If the religious situation is changing, then we must expect corresponding change in the intellectual vehicle of a tradition participating in the situation. In this case we are evaluating the situational change in terms of convergence, and hence the change in the conceptualization of the structure and function of theology must reflect convergence; concretely, it must recast theology as an instrument of communication among diverse yet participating traditions. Hence a "new theology" is in continuity with an older conceptualization insofar as *we* expect to be in continuity with the tradition served by the "old theology."

To integrate our yes-and-no answer, we must recall how theology developed historically for Judaism, Christianity and Islam. Central to the development in each instance has been the intellectual need to relate to a general understanding of the world around us a religious experience and content which is revelational in character. That is, these Traditions assert that *somehow* in the historic process there is an occurrence of transhistoric significance, and this must be seen as being meaningful (again *somehow*) in continuity with all that is of historic significance. Theological systems have arisen to meet the challenge of those *somehows*. To see the force of such a development and, hopefully, to see also the basis of continuity between "old" and "new" theology, we must understand how theologizing and theologies emerge in the histories of Judaism, Christianity and Islam. (As will become evident through even a brief examination, the theologizing and theologies of Judaism, Christianity and Islam represent quite different intellectual experiences for each Tradition, however much they might appear to have in common.)

All three religious Traditions participate in the Graeco-Roman intellectual heritage, which is the source of both the word "theology" and its position in the disciplines of knowledge. Aristotle recognized three branches of theoretical philosophy: mathematical, physical and theological.[1] For him theology was the inquiry concerning the gods (*theologos, theologein*) and this branch of philosophy, drawing upon the mythological narratives of the gods as handed down by tradition, represented the pre-scientific stage of the reflection on the things of reality. Theology, thus, did not concern itself with truth or falsity or any attempt to derive knowledge from a body of sacred tradition (of sacred texts or their equivalent as materials within a known historic context), but rather it represented the historical depth and genesis of the contemporary as this could be seen in "proto-philosophical" symbolic statements of the primitives.

While accepting this notion in part, the Stoics distinguished three divisions in theology which allowed it to assume the status of a discipline of study in its own right rather than being simply an historical preamble to the mathematical and physical. *Mythical theology* dealt with the materials in tradition concerning the gods and their worship and, as with Aristotle, was narrative in character. *Civil theology* dealt with the practices of religion as these related concretely to the nature and function of society; in certain respects civil theology contained elements of a primitive sociology, especially as treated by such Roman theorists as Cicero.[2] *Natural theology,* however, moved beyond the mythic-symbolic traditions and their functional position within society to a quest for a verifiable account of the divine, both in itself and in human-cosmic relationship. This division of natural theology provides the disciplinary model for the formation of early Christian theology.

It is of the greatest importance to our present interest to note that the continuity between the Stoic discipline of natural theology and that of Tertullian, Augustine and the other early formulators of Christian theological discipline is in terms of systematization, notwithstanding radical difference in both the materials of the content and the evaluation of those materials (Graeco-Roman mythic-symbolic traditions not structured within an historic context as opposed to a Christian revelational tradition completely integral to history). Corresponding interest on the part of contemporary Hellenistic Judaists parallels this important distinction between disciplinary systematization and the content of the religious tradition to be systematized. In each instance, a concept of an intellectual discipline which had taken shape within the Greek non-revelational tradition was found appropriate for the formulation of intellectual meaning of revelational traditions. In the very origins of Christian and Judaic theology, therefore, we have ample demonstration that theology precisely as a discipline is not adequately defined as "the science of revelation" or the like. The Western tendency to bind together theology and revelation is far too restrictive.   .

That theology represents an attempt to systematize necessitates the employment of some coherent instrument. For both early Christian and Judaic theologians this naturally meant a philosophical instrument, and of the major structures available at that time both accepted Neoplatonism as the most suitable, given the overall character of the materials of their traditions. Neoplatonism itself had developed a world-view concerning the foundations of religious notions conceived of as natural to man. Following philosophical form and adhering to philosophical methods this systematization allowed Christians and Judaists to build upon an accepted natural framework of values, integrating their commitments to revelational history with it, gaining insight on the one hand into the intellectual meaning of their faith and on the other being able to extend its significance coherently to all that was embraced philosophically by Neoplatonism, and in the same terms and with the same meanings.

Philosophical theology[3] quickly established itself for both Traditions as the indispensable vehicle of understanding and communication, popular as well as specialized. Thus, Clement of Alexandria (identifying the basic significance of theology with revelation) could say that philosophy truly so called *is* theology.[4] For Augustine the identity between the revelational tradition and theology had become so complete that he broke away from the original Stoic tripartite concept of mythical-civil-natural theology and opposed mythology to natural theology (of course with the value presuppositions of false religion and true religion).[5]

For Philo and other early Judaists philosophy and theology (as with Christians, seen as essentially revelational) were to be identified and projected backwards in history for a proper understanding of the origins of the revelational tradition. Thus, Philo viewed all the Biblical prophets as theologians, and for him Moses was the theologian *par excellence*. This theological identity also permitted the Hellenist Judaist to reverse the effect and see Moses and the prophets as philosophers in the sense of the Greek intellectual tradition and thereby establish Moses as both the greatest theologian and the greatest philosopher! Under Philo's influence the development of allegorical exegesis led inevitably to a curious philosophizing of scriptural texts with two contradictory results: the imposition of philosophical meanings upon non-philosophical compositions produced an esoteric nominalism, and it also inevitably reestablished the older Stoic relationship of mythological and natural theology—with the Biblical materials as de-historicized myths.

In developing theological systems within the framework of Graeco-Roman civilization, both Judaists and Christians were consciously apologists. For Judaism the task was to relate the tradition to the secular world so that the Judaist could participate in it while remaining within the primary identity of the covenanted people set apart, and to do this with intellectual respectability. For Christianity the task was one of survival and conversion. However we are to interpret the opposition to the world spoken of so often and so forcefully in the Christian Scriptures, early Christians soon saw themselves as transforming the civilization of this world, Christianizing it, making it over into a City of God. In this process the decision was made at the beginning to "baptize" the philosophers and all that was compatible in the pre-Christian intellectual tradition.[6]

II

Conceived of by Christians as a science of revelation, *theologia* meant the teaching of God, in the confined sense of *this* teaching (i.e., revelation of divine truth) *by* God rather than in the broader sense of teaching concerning God. The medieval theologians in fact rarely refer to *theologia* to designate their interest but speak of *sacra doctrina,* and this sacred teaching of course is the body of Christian doctrine. This is thought of as a specific gathering of doctrinal materials, referred to classically as the *deposit of Faith.* It is presumed that there is a set limit to this deposit, usually expressed as all those truths revealed to and within the Church before the death of the last of the original Apostles and received by the Church under apostolic authority. Most doctrinal elements were given explicit statement in the body of canonical literature designated as Sacred Scripture, though other elements were maintained in an oral tradition and were witnessed to during the next several centuries, especially in the writings of the Church Fathers. (Although this distinction between a written Biblical tradition and an oral tradition became a major issue of the Sixteenth Century Reformation crisis, all the development of systematic theology from the Patristic period to the late Middle Ages is based upon it.)

Although theology might be thought of as *sacra doctrina* in terms of the presumed origin of the materials of the tradition, nonetheless the disciplinary development was not basically exegetical in form, the primary reason for this being the fact that the materials took their significance from the existential experience of Christ as an historic being and not from an idea or principle. However the "stuff" of Christian theology might be conceived, the reality of the historic Jesus stands at the core of all that Christianity is and hence, in the last analysis, theology must study *him* rather than *it.* Because from the beginning Christians have expressed their experience of him in both human and divine terms integrally, the fundamental theological issues are inevitably Christ-centered.

Justin Martyr as an early apologist-theologian illustrates this in the sequence of his interests. As he asserts that the predicate *theos* belongs properly to the historic Jesus of Nazareth as Messiah, he establishes the God-Man experience and its interpretation as the center of theological systematization. This, in turn, necessitates a formulation of relationship within Divinity, leading to Trinitarian statements as the expression of the primitive Father-Son-Spirit distinctions. Christian theology, therefore, must orient toward the problems of what can and must be said about Divinity as within the God-Man experience, and also must orient toward the human historical relationships of man-man and man-God since the God-Man experience is conscious as historical and not mythic-symbolic, and this *incarnation* is conscious as universally purposive (specifically, *redemptive*). From Justin onward to the Middle Ages theology is geared to this exploration. Especially in the early Patristic period we can see this development as a creative process in which the religious experiential tradition is subjected to a progressive systematization with all the tensions of probing and testing as one problem after another is uncovered, subjected to discipline and evaluated.

As we consider the state of theology in the Middle Ages we can observe that a marked change has taken place. The emphasis for the most part has shifted from the earlier creativity to in-depth exploration of the formulated doctrine. The great problems (and their basic solutions) seem to have been established. Creativity is now a matter of elaboration and the explicitation of what is implicitly contained in the settled areas. At this point a controversy of far-reaching importance takes place between Bernard of Clairvaux and Abelard concerning the ultimate function of theology.

For Bernard theologizing itself is an act of religion. It is the intellectual dimension of the act of faith and must begin as a quest of spirit rather than of the mind, the mind being the instrument only and in no way imposing any need of its own upon the undertaking, apart from a receptivity in such understanding as is achieved. Bernard's theology is fundamentally Biblical, presuming the sacred texts to be of themselves the revealing statements of truth and wisdom from which the mind seeks to learn. The pursuit of the theologian issues in prayerful reaffirmation of Faith, and ideally in mystical contemplation. Bernard's concept of the function of theology is the direct outgrowth of his monastic experience with its heavy emphasis on *lectio divina,* the worshipful-contemplative reading of the sacred text and the Patristic interpretations and commentaries. It is a religious act in which one *listens* to the prophetic witness to wisdom and then attempts to bring one's own consciousness into conformity with it. The *sacra doctrina* and the *lectio divina* appear to be the two complementing and integral dimensions of theology whose substance, then, is the wisdom of God in the body of sacred teaching, and whose activity and function are conscious and responsive worship in the act of listening to the divine reading.

For Abelard this monastic theological tradition subverts all the objective value in the functioning of the human mind. He insists that the theological quest is first of all an intellectual one, which certainly can be expected to serve the spirit, but which itself is not an act of religion and does not begin and end in worship and contemplation. As properly an act of the mind, theologizing must be subject to the demands of logic and the discipline of language. The sacred texts and reflections on them are material for theological consideration, but that takes place under the rigorous requirements of a coherent (philosophical) system. The success of Abelard in this controversy established theology as a proper intellectual discipline open to the dynamics of conceivably any philosophical system, and called upon the philosophical theologian to act creatively upon the stuff of the religious tradition.

(An unfortunate aftermath of this settlement, however, has been the progressive detachment from theology of all aspects of the contemplative. Rather than becoming simply autonomous dimensions of the dynamics of the religious tradition—each meaningful to the other within the appropriate disciplinary limits—the theological and the contemplative in Christianity have become dissociated. In the decline of scholasticism of the Fourteenth and Fifteenth Centuries, theology as an intellectual discipline became opposed to "mystical theology"—which itself was almost indefinitely subdivided into independent categories, such as ascetical theology, and the like. Theology and disciplined mysticism both suffered in consequence, the former from the danger of losing realistic touch with the tradition as a living religious tradition of experience [and hence Fourteenth Century nominalism], the latter from the danger of anti-intellectualism.)

For Thomas Aquinas and those of his generation, the recovery of the central works of Aristotle, lost to the West until retransmitted through Muslim civilization, meant a totally new creativity. With a new philosophical system as their instrument they set about to erect a radically new systematization of Christian theology. To be sure *sacra doctrina* now included all the materials of the tradition, but the theologians' own creativity entered the tradition, modified it significantly, asking questions, raising new issues and formulating statements according to the suggestiveness of the philosophical instrument—beyond what the sacred texts and earlier commentaries called for and perhaps allowed. The Thomist demonstration of the applicability of the Aristotelian system as an instrument of systematization can be seen as the foundation of Christian theological pluralism, whether the instrument is philosophical or empirical. Actual theological pluralism emerges in the Post-Reformation attempts to reconstitute a coherent understanding of Christianity with an ever more rapidly changing world. At present the emergence of the empirical sciences as radically new sources of disciplined knowledge seems to call for an even more creative pluralism.

III

Philo and the other Alexandrian Hellenists in their attempt to synthesize the tradition of the Torah and the prophetic writings with Neoplatonic philosophy exposed Judaism to the danger of losing its consciousness of the living covenant relationship. With Moses as a mystical philosopher, allegory and symbol could easily obscure the gulf separating Greek and Semitic thoughts and traditions. However, the collapse of the Alexandrian Jewish community effectively ended this line of development.

In the period between the Sixth and Eleventh Centuries, Judaism constructed the permanent foundations of its theological tradition. The first important work of systematic theology, Saadia's *Sefer Haemunoth Vehadeoth* (or, Book of Beliefs and Opinions) of 933 A.D., marked a new kind of study of the tradition beyond the recitation of the opinions of chains of authorities. It reflected contemporary Islamic theological interests, arrangements, treatments of material, etc., and thus participated in a partially shared intellectual tradition of Graeco-Roman origin.

Maimonides, the greatest of the classic Jewish theologians, established the disciplinary character of Judaic theology firmly by following Aristotle's identification of theology with metaphysics. For Maimonides theology had two clear functions within a religious tradition: to inquire into immaterial beings (God, angels), and to establish the underlying causes of things belonging to the other sciences. Hence, his work covered systematically the formulation of articles of faith in terms of philosophical categories and the development of the theory of law and ethics reflecting the commitment to the Torah, as well as the popularization of the understanding of Judaic faith.

Jewish theologians from Saadia to Maimonides (and for some time after) worked within the structure of Muslim Mediterranean and Near Eastern culture. The place of the Jewish community within Islam was at least intellectually secure, and both drew directly from the older Graeco-Roman intellectual tradition which was the immediate inheritance of the Muslim conquest of the Byzantine East. While Western Europe awaited the rediscovery of the lost philosophical tradition (to be mediated by Muslim civilization through southern Italy and the Iberian Caliphate), both Judaism and Islam developed a variety of theological systems on Greek philosophical models.

The paramount intellectual task of Muslim theologians has been the interpretation of the text of the Qur'ān, and while there are inevitably resemblances to the interests of Judaic and Chris-

tian theologians as they also attempt to deal with textual interpretations of received scriptures, Qur'anic interpretation re-
sponds to a special inner force of faithfulness to the text as itself a
portion of the subsistent Divine Wisdom. The Prophet was a *reci-
ter* of the sacred words, not one inspired to write simply his own
words which would somehow contain and transmit revelational
truth. There is thus a very real sacramental or "incarnational"
quality to the Qur'anic text which resists an easy distinction between a human mediating element and a divine truth-reality behind or beyond it.

The rise of schools of interpretation, therefore, has most often
meant the development of religious sects divided from one another by conflicting commitments. Within the first century of
Islam school-sects emerged, not simply from popular or philosophical speculation, but from the inner drive of the sacred text
to be seen as totally significant to the world being called to faithfulness by the revelation. Because the actual statements of the
Qur'ān must somehow be taken as worded and must be the practical norms of lived-out faithfulness, the statements must be able
to be interpreted logically and coherently in their literalness.
Hence the earliest Muslim theologians sought systematization in
terms of reason and logic rather than the traditions of teachings
(though these are of the greatest importance both in establishing
the context of the Qur'anic statements and in the application of
the Qur'ān ethically and legally to concrete life situations).

The earliest school-sect was Mu'tazilism, founded by Wāṣil b.
'Aṭā' (A.D. 699–748). It applied a test of logic to Qur'anic revelation producing a very different picture of the Faith from that of
the original believers. A theory of indeterminism was educed
from the affirmation of the absolute Justice of God; if man was
commanded to act responsibly then man must be the proper author of his own acts. From the affirmation that God was not contained in any place, it must be that there is no beatific vision—
beholding the Godhead "here" individually. From the affirmation of Divine Omniscience, it must be that there are no recording angels since God Himself knows everything. Most important

of all, Mu'tazilists concluded that the Qur'ān is a created speech of Allah, coming into existence with the Prophethood of Muhammad.

Under succeeding teachers Mu'tazilism became clearly a philosophical theology whose interests and categories were intellectually derived rather than prompted by the sacred text, as this was no longer regarded as a divine subsistence. Thus, for example, the conceptualization of the singularity and unity of God's Nature brought al-Naẓẓām (d. 845 A.D.) to deny a Will in God —to speak of Divine Will was nothing more than to affirm that creation was according to Divine Knowledge. Influenced through Plotinus by Neoplatonism, Mu'ammar (d. 842? A.D.) denied Knowledge in God—God's nature as absolutely One precludes all attributes. Thamāmah (d. 828 A.D.) under Aristotelian influence concluded that the universe is uncreated and eternal, necessitated by the Nature of God.[7]

This type of theological development begins with logic problems arising in the sacred text insofar as it is not a systematized document. Historically in contact with Greek philosophical thought as a native part of their heritage (a point we tend to forget when we think of the formation of Near Eastern Islamic Civilization in the century following Muhammad), early Muslim theologians soon sought the basis for an intellectual approach to the text which, paradoxically, tended to undercut the authority of the text. In pursuit of a cultural integration of Islam and Greek-Byzantine Civilization, the early 'Abbasid Caliphs—especially al-Ma'mūn—encouraged Arabic translations of the Greek classics and the fusion of a philosophic rationalism with Qur'anic interpretation. With the proliferation of schools and sects with their rationalist subversion of the integrity of the Qur'ān as the direct self-revelation of Divine Wisdom, the Tenth and Eleventh Centuries witnessed a severe reaction. Philosophical theology as such was to be rejected. And not only was an ultra-literalism of the Qur'ān insisted upon, but many asserted that the Qur'ān was uncreated. For them the content of the revelation, the text as it stood and the language itself must be accepted as always existing and consubstantial with the Godhead. A distinction was made between the Qur'ān which had come through the Prophet and the infinite Heavenly Qur'ān, in that the former was but a portion of the latter, but as transmitted to mankind the earthly Qur'ān was simply not part of creation.

The effect on the concept of theology of such a reaction can be seen in this citation given by M. M. Sharif:

. . . . Malik bin Anas said: "God's settling Himself firmly upon His Throne is known, the how of it is unknown; belief in it is obligatory; and questioning about it is an innovation." Any speculation about sacred things (especially as contained expressly in the Qur'ān) was considered an innovation. Every dogma was to be believed without raising the question how or why (*bila kaifa*).[8]

However, there was also a more moderate reaction against Mu'tazilite rationalism. The rise of Aṣh'arism under al-Aṣh'arī (d. c. 941) established philosophical theology on a firmly orthodox base in insisting on the integrity of the Qur'ān while rejecting both rationalist and fundamentalist approaches. For Aṣh'arists, Islam is not opposed to the use of reason; in fact, a rationalization of faith is a necessity. Revelation, not pure reason, is the foundation of Islam, but of necessity revelation must be *understood* if one is called to a living faithfulness. Thus conscious faithfulness is to be rationalized from revelation. Using the fundamentalists' weapons against them, Aṣh'arists drew attention to the fact that the Prophet was silent on the issue of the ultimate nature of the Qur'ān; thus to assert that the Qur'ān is uncreated is just as much an innovation as to assert that it is created! Following a middle course between rationalists and fundamentalists, the resolution of the problem was proposed in a distinction: the Qur'ān in its expression in words is created while in its inner meanings it is uncreated.

The success of this middle way became the source of an intense development of Muslim philosophical theology. With the establishment of a complementarity between faith and reason, the de-

velopment of Muslim scholasticism took place and, though limited, became one of the very few positive contact points between
Islam and Christianity. The works of al-Kindi (801–873 A.D.),
al-Farabi (870–950 A.D.) and Ibn Sina (980–1037 A.D.) were especially influential on the formation of medieval Christian scholasticism in the following two centuries.

IV

Even this brief recitation of the origins of theological discipline
within Judaism, Christianity and Islam reveals several fundamental factors proper to an historic understanding of theology—
both as to its past and potential for the future.

First, in each case any interest in developing what could be
called theology arose from two sources. Given the commitment to
a religious content which must be asserted to be transhistorical
(however further one would wish to specify the meaning of "revelation"), this content must be related coherently to the rest of
what man knows. And if this historical dimension is approached
by men in any sort of systematized way, then necessarily the coherence of the transhistorical with it must be in the same terms.
The alternative is to be content with leaving the religious content
unrelated. (In actuality, this alternative is theoretical only; any
attempt to *understand* the religious content—and this is unavoidable even if merely rudimentary—will mean understanding in
the way we seek to understand other things.) Thus, theologizing
of some sort, however primitive it may be, will inevitably take
place, and we can see for Judaism, Christianity and Islam how
small the interval is between the beginnings of serious theological
development and the final laying down of the experiential materials of the tradition.[9]

The particular structures for theology in all three Traditions
have their source directly in Greek philosophy, especially in Neoplatonism and Aristotelianism. This was inevitable in the circumstances. For Christians, as for the most part members of the

Graeco-Roman Civilization, there was the necessity of making the Tradition in its initial formative process native to their way of life. For Judaists and Muslims as they either moved into Graeco-Roman Civilization or absorbed it into a new cultural synthesis, there was the need to demonstrate continuity of intellectual values.

Although each Tradition is fully committed to the reality of a transhistorical Presence in phenomenal history—and as integrated, not alien—the nature of this Presence *as experienced* and as this experience is *shared* is quite different in each case. If we think of each Tradition in terms of revelation as scriptural revelation they are very similar—covenantal Torah, Gospels, and Qur'ān— differing markedly in contents (in spite of many shared elements), but the same in the sense of presenting "revealed truths" as the stuff for conscious faithfulness. As scriptural revelation they simply compete for acceptance insofar as one is called upon to recognize the authenticity of the contents. But if the transhistorical Presence witnessed by each Tradition is thought of in terms of *what happens* at the proposed point of contact between the transhistorical and the historical, the meaning of *revelation* in each case is radically different. (Before proceeding, these cautions must be taken into account. It is hazardous to attempt to put these "what happens" into words, especially a few words, but it must be done to see how different they really are. These statements are vastly oversimplified, and two of the three are written from the point of view of an outsider who must see things in terms of his known commitment. The selection of one dimension of content does not exclude others, but is made to point up contrast—as well as to suggest complementarity. With these and similar limitations in mind we can mark off some differences in the "happenings.")

For Judaism, the Torah embodying the Covenant witnesses the radical interiorization of a people—drawn together from scattered origins, called to a common life whose significance somehow is always in a tension of destruction and survival. The vision of human life is to be sought "inside"—within the experience of community, of family, of individual as meaningful only when related in a sense of origin (Covenant) which contains destiny (promise).

For Christianity, the Gospel proclamation witnesses to the existial uniting of the transhistorical and historical within the reality of an actual man, the historic Jesus, and the extension of this union to every man through him. The whole condition of mankind and the cosmos is thus in a continuing process of transformation, with the experience of liberation, fulfillment and the immediacy of Divinity integral to humanity.

For Islam, the Qur'ān is the call to faithfulness in the Absolute revealed in the fullness within the Will creative of universal order, a Will both purposive and compassionate. In this Will man individually and socially experiences his existence as from God, who loves him because he has undertaken the Trust of Faith, the God who thus loves man's doings and requires him to establish faithfulness as the loving response of everyone and everything to the Creator. Islam, thus, calls mankind to build a way of life and a world fitted to be the universal temple of God in which Divine Order is manifested according to the command of Revelation.

However faulty and limited these renditions of some of the dimensions of the revelational happenings certainly are, we should be able to recognize that the differences in the Traditions are not basically in terms of a content of the sacred texts. Of course the texts differ, but precisely insofar as they are attempts to put into words differing transhistorical-historical contact experiences.

All of this should stir us to recognize a very important implication. Historic theological systems have, for the most part, been occupied with systematizing the religious traditions in terms of scriptural revelation. That is, the first task has been to apply reason to the foundational mass of *ideas* in the tradition. Since the *ideas* are themselves reflective of a very specific experience or constellation of experiences, should not theology see its first task as the systematic relation of the *experiencing(s)* to everything else? This might seem to be a merely nominal distinction; whichever priority were acknowledged, there should be no *practical* difference in the outcome of the systematizing since to get at the experience process one must work through the actual expression integral to it. For example, would either make any difference in the need for Christians to formulate a specific range of Christological doctrines to express the experiencing of man and God in union in the historic Jesus?

There would be a difference. The theological object *could not* be treated as static—as a content of "stuff"—if priority rested with the process of experiencing. The contents of the texts as recording the transhistorical-historical contact experience can only reflect a chosen moment. To be sure, this should be of unique value as it inevitably involves the never to be repeated origin-moment. But if revelation is not limited to that point of history but involves as well the process of experiencing-what-continues-to-happen, then theology will have a different form and content, to relate the dynamics of an on-going transhistoric-historic experiencing.

Participants in these Traditions must make an explicit choice. They must limit the significance of the Tradition to a repetition of the selected historic moment if revelation is static and not processual. If they do, theology is an exegetical enterprise only, whose purpose is to provide an absolutely accurate rendition of the original ideas, practices, etc., to make possible their repetition in the present. The uniqueness of the past revelational moment and that of the on-going present are thus merely incidental to each other, and no rational relationship beyond this is called for or allowed. As seen earlier with Muslim fundamentalists, any speculation about sacred things must be considered innovation and belief in what is already established must be without question of how or why. In the history of Christianity (including some contemporary developments) this attempt to live theologically within the supposed confines of a moment in the past has led, over and over again, to a serious rejection of the experienced present (hence the sacred-secular antipathy, which reduces the contemporary reality to an evil to be rejected—"worldliness"—or to an instrumental expedient of value only for a "higher" end—

the building stones of a New Jerusalem); or, it has led to nominalist sophistry and casuistry, maintaining the formulae of words while imposing meanings having but tenuous connection with the original meaning intended by the writer (hence, scriptural allegoricalism, extravagant use of *sensus plenior* by hindsight, and so forth).

V

A concept of theology which takes seriously the on-going process of experiencing as integral to the significance of the point of origin necessarily rejects any notion of repetition. The historic moment of origination of the religious tradition must be taken seriously, for it is genetic not only in the sense of starting things off but also in seminally setting the basic structure and direction of all future growth. This does not mean that the future is fully contained in its past and simply unfolds deterministically. But it does mean that the first level of reality in any tradition is the ultimate norm for actual continuity: it unavoidably sets limits to the kinds of development which can take place and still maintain continuity. Negatively, the norm of origination tells us when something new is not in continuity with the tradition (and thus is itself the potential origination of a new tradition) when the new development does not share *any* of the constituting content at the foundation of the experience process.

(This notion can be stated much more easily than put into practice. Thus, is Christianity actually discontinuous with Judaism? Is there no sharing of the constituting content? Is Islam discontinuous with Judaism and Christianity? Are Hinduism and Buddhism both continuous descendants of earlier Brahminism? Is Buddhism a heresy of Hinduism? And so on. As we can see, we are dealing with a subtle factor which itself can be a source of new dynamism in interreligious theological relationships.)

Any revelational tradition presumes that the "contact" of the transhistorical and historical is not a momentary collision with nothing more than shock-wave aftermath. On the contrary, each historic revelation is supposed henceforth to be totally integral to all that continues to happen. To take that expectation seriously it is not enough to "read" the past as the present, find in the present that its essentials "already exist," or any such evasion. The present must be accepted as genuinely *new* (which is just what it seems to be!) and we must seek to recognize integral genetic development in a continuum of past-present-future, in which the integrity of each allows us to penetrate ever more deeply the significance of each as processual. And following this choice also brings the theologian the comforting benefit of freedom from embarrassment in that no longer must he "make things fit," subvert originally intended meanings, or submit to concessions wrung from him by advances in human insight. Rather, he is committed to a process of development, an integral continuity in which real newness is regularly expected and which consequently sets his task as one of continuing reformation. There is risk—of losing contact at any point with the genesis of the tradition and thus becoming totally discontinuous—but there is a greater risk in attempting to fulfill a commitment to the static repetition of the past—the inevitable discovery that the nominalism has evacuated all meaning and the tradition has been eroded to a fragile, perhaps lifeless, shell.

Returning to the issue at the beginning of this chapter, we should now be in a position to see validity in extending theology as an intellectual discipline to non-Western Traditions. The identification of Judaic, Christian and Muslim theologies with Graeco-Roman philosophical traditions has been appropriate to the historic context of Western (including Near Eastern) Civilization; however, such identification is not essential to theology as such. More recent theological development demonstrates that the discipline readily employs any philosophical instrument as its means of systematization, and further, there is no reason why an empirical instrument cannot be used. That Judaism, Christianity and Islam are overtly revelational in character has meant that theology has dealt, properly, with the systematization of the par-

ticular revelational tradition and the relation of it to the phenomenal. Once again, the identification of theologizing with a
revelational commitment is contextual, not essential. If we take
as our basic definition of theology *the systematization of man's experience of definitive relationship,* any tradition centered upon the experience of definitiveness can be theologized according to any one, or
several, of the available philosophical or empirical instruments,
and according to the proper character of its content and life-
form.

Should non-Western Traditions develop theological systems?
And should Western theologians approach the non-Western Traditions theologically (rather than, at best, through a peripheral
and ancillary use of cullings from historical and comparative
studies)? Unquestionably, yes, if we hope to communicate creatively with each other and with the intellectual structures of the
world around us and within which we must live. If we look
closely we will see that actually the non-Westerners already have
the theological experience. We have only to recall Sankara and
the Indian scholastic philosophy, the linguistic analysis (of a
uniquely Chinese sort) of the Confucian commentaries, and the
like, to recognize that systematization of definitive experience is
not unknown outside the West.

We are required, then, to decide whether or not we wish to
communicate seriously (with all the expectation of something
further happening to us all), and devise commutually the appropriate means. The emergence of the empirical disciplines as dominant intellectual forms throughout the world as secular convergence takes place seems to indicate that systematization for
religious convergence should be structured in terms of empirical
theology. Thus, the newness of the religious situation would be
matched appropriately by an intellectual newness, unfettered
from the divisiveness of past culture prejudices and wide open to
an undetermined future.

THE
REVELATIONAL
IN
RELIGION

I

As in the case with many of the central categories of the study of religious experience, *revelation* or the *revelational* as both a term and a meaning has been defined exclusively within the context of Western experience, Judaic, Christian and Muslim.[1] In the previous chapter we accepted this situation without questioning it. But it must be questioned.

It is fairly widely taken for granted without challenge that the Western Traditions alone can lay claim to be characterized as revelational in origin and function. Putting aside any question as to whether or not any or all of them are in fact revelational, we must ask why other Traditions are presumed to be non-revelational. Westerners regard Buddhism, for example, as clearly non-revelational—and Buddhists typically seem to agree. If we review the basis for the judgment we find in such an instance that the presentation of the category *revelation* does indeed exclude Buddhism, and practically any other Eastern religion. This can mean either of two things: either whatever the revelational properly is

147

actually is limited to the Western experience, or the revelational has been conceived of much too narrowly in that the Western experience as culture-bound has innocently given rise to presuppositions of exclusion which are unrealistic in the light of the full range of religious phenomena. Obviously, any exploration of the question must be addressed to the latter alternate.

At the outset it is interesting how much evidence of dissatisfaction with limiting revelation to the West we can discover within Christian theology. To be sure until recently it has been evidence of an indirect sort, but consistent in its implication. It can be put very simply: Christian theologians have often been made uneasy by discerning (however superficially) elements in the other Traditions which to the Christian look like they should have a revelational basis (usually because they look like "Christian elements"). It does not matter that such elements are most often accounted for in an insensitive way and with makeshift theological devices—vestiges of a "primitive revelation" (pre-Noah, or the like), or supposed borrowings from Christianity, or a special revelational preparation for an approaching evangelization. We have already seen some of these in passing (the early apologists' "baptizing" of the Greek philosophers, sybilline prophets, Ricci's accommodation of Confucianism, and so on). Apart from exhibiting varieties of reductionism, these are instances of experiential recognition of at least some aspects in other Traditions that appear that they should have a revelational basis (origin and/or function). This *can* indicate that the theological notion of revelation has been too narrow in construction and the theologians recognize this implicitly in the need to devise theological gadgets.

Naturally the cultural context in which the religious experience takes place and finds expression circumscribes the range of meaning any category can be given. This cultural relativity in words and meanings, though limiting, is the only condition whereby the experience-expression can be relevant to historical situations. As real people are this or that *sort* of people, so the reality of religious experience-expression naturally enough must be a corresponding *sort*. Of the several types of limitations imposed by this fact of cultural context, the one of interest to us here is the most subtle: the usual inability of the participant in the religious-cultural context to recognize consciously that there is such a limitation. The theological gadgets devised to account for that which has been pre-excluded from the identified historic revelational situation are the evidences for the unconscious recognition that the conscious definition of the revelational is inadequate.

There is another line of evidence of the problem created by cultural relativity even more impressive than that of the gadgets. Judaism, Christianity and Islam have most often centered their concern with the revelational upon sacred books. Each Tradition has scriptures, and anything approaching an "orthodox" attitude in each presupposes an essential link between the writing of the books and the occurrence of revelation. Putting aside the particular questions of inspiration, inerrancy and the like, and also putting aside the judgments each Tradition makes about the revelational condition of the others' books, the identification of a revelational situation with the production and preservation of sacred writings should create at least theological embarrassment upon noting that "non-revelational" Traditions also have books regarded as sacred and as essentially linked to the shared experience.

Apart from lifting out elements of "primitive revelation" or the like from these sacred texts, the theologians' solution to the dilemma has been simple: these are not to be regarded as sacred books or scriptures; for the progressive theologian they may indeed be "holy" and worthy of "reverence" for some reason and in some way, but they are not *Sacred Scripture* in the proper sense. This judgment of course rests upon a presupposition: only certain received writings are *Scripture*. And this presupposition itself rests upon the implicit evaluation of absolutized exclusiveness for the Tradition of the theologian.

The theological argument is often filled out with another unchallenged culture-bound type of judgment. A self-evident *quality* in the received Scripture is appealed to as a contrast to the "sacred writings of other people." Thus, the four Gospels are pointed to by Christians as unique in contents and expression, as is the Qur'ān by Muslims and the Torah by Judaists. And in each instance even a casual acquaintance with the writings supports such a view—each is unique, different substantially from the others, and from all others regardless of Tradition. The problem is that this assertion can and should be made for all of the bodies of sacred writings: each really is unique. This very fact attracts our attention to them, and it is clear that those who participate in the Tradition identifiable with this or that Scripture read those books as they can read no others.

When it is argued that the issue is not merely uniqueness as such, but the entire meaning and thrust of the writings whereby they have a unique significance for man, once again we must agree but also point to the unresolved evaluation of *difference* and *relativity. These books* seem uniquely significant for man but not *those,* is a judgment that takes for granted that there is no convergent significance of no-longer-separate Traditions for one another. And the *exclusive* unique significance now still experienced in our separations means not that the other books do not speak significantly, but they *as yet* do not speak *to me.*

II

Much of the current Christian theological concern with the identification of the revelational with the Scriptures received within the Christian Church has been shaped by the relatively recent Reformation crisis with the particular emphasis placed (in any one of several ways) upon the words of the texts. Whether one adhered to a Protestant conviction of the Scripture in itself as the sole norm of Faith or to a Catholic conviction of Scripture and Apostolic Tradition as interpreted by the authority of the Church, one could not separate the revelational and Scripture. And as explicitly one could not admit to the corpus of Scripture any but the already received documents, implicitly one could not admit anything further to the "content" of revelation, nor extend the scope of the revelational to include ranges of religious experience not directly assimilable to the "Judaeo-Christian."

Yet the examination of pre-Reformation theological history provides us with conceptualizations of revelation which do not admit of this type of narrowness. This is not to say that there is an explicit extension of the revelational beyond the accommodations discussed previously. But there are structures which at least implicitly open up the range of meaning beyond the confines of a closed religious system.

The theological tradition formed in the experiential emphasis of the early Greek Fathers, carried forward into the Western Church by Augustine, and during the high Middle Ages systematized in the Franciscan branch of scholasticism proposes a potentially open-ended significance for revelation. For Bonaventure all of phenomenal existence is to be seen as coming forth from God and as in the process of returning to Him. Thus, in the *Itinerarium Mentis in Deum*[2] man is depicted as on a journey as a pilgrim through a world by no means alien to him or to God his goal. The world in everything that composes it reflects God in countless ways and so aids man in his quest for return.

For Bonaventure there are two symbols of primary importance, *mirror* and *book*, which portray the reflectivity of creation. First, all of reality shows forth God as in a mirror which draws man on in an ever intensifying light as man step by step approaches union with God. Thus, the cosmos is a mirror, or *speculum*, for God makes it possible for man to *speculate* or see-contemplate the reality of God as this is reflected in literally everything. And so the universe as a mirror is the basis for man's *knowing* something intellectually of God and for his *beholding* God in religious experience.

In the light of the traditional Christian linking of the revelational with the Scriptures, Bonaventure's other symbol of the *book* implies an even more open meaning for revelation than does the mirror. At the outset we should note that the book symbol is not focused on the sense of a book as an object and hence static, but on the process of *reading a book*. As with the mirror symbol, we are concerned with man as actively *in via* and so *moving*. To read the book rightly enlightens man so he can progress toward his goal of union with God.

In terms of the ultimate relation of cosmos to God the book is actually two-fold:

There are two books: one written within, which is the eternal art and wisdom of God; and the other written without, that is the material world.[3]

In terms of the unfolding of history as God reveals Himself to man, the book is found to be three-fold:

. . . . the foundation of the whole Christian Faith . . . has a triple testimony . . . considered from the standpoint of three books: the book of creation, the book of scripture and the book of life. . . . The book of creation . . . first shown to our senses gives a two-fold testimony. . . . For every creature is either a vestige, only, of God such as are corporeal natures, or also an image of God as are intellectual creatures.[4]

It is important to note that this three-fold book symbol is being employed by Bonaventure to situate the process of the revelation of God as Trinity which he identifies doctrinally as "the foundation of the whole Christian Faith"! So we have a pointed indication of how much weight he intends to place upon expressions which locate the revelational process in a much wider range than that supposedly bounded by the texts of sacred books. And even more explicit is his enumeration of the three books, with the book of the scripture having its relevance between the book of creation (as the book written without) and the book of life (as the book written within):

Now this double testimony of the book of nature [that is, the testimony of creation as *vestiges* and as *images*] was efficacious in the state in which nature was created, when this book was not obscure and the eye of man had not been clouded. But when man's eye was clouded by sin, that mirror was made obscure and dark,[5] and the ear of his interior intelligence became deaf to hearing that testimony.[6] And therefore Divine Providence planned and provided for the testimony of another book, namely the book of Scripture, which was published by divine revelation. . . .[7]

But the third book, the book of life, *goes beyond* the book of scripture and the book of creation:

But since "not all obey the Gospel," and this truth [that is, the doctrine of the Trinity] is above reason, therefore Divine Wisdom provided an eternal testimony, which indeed is the book of life. Now this book of life through itself and in itself explicitly and expressly gives irresistible testimony . . . to those who with face unveiled see God in the *homeland* [that is, at the completion of man's journey of return to God], but on the *way* it gives testimony according to the influence of the light which the soul is capable of in the wayfarer's state. . . . It enlightens in two ways, namely, through an innate light, and through an infused light. . . .

. . . . For through a light placed naturally within man by God and stamped as the light of the divine countenance, each one's own reason dictates to himself that concerning the first principle we ought to think most highly and most piously. . . . And on this point Christians, Jews, Saracens and also heretics agree. . . .

If, then, we ask—what moves one to believe this, whether, namely, Scripture or miracles or grace or eternal truth itself?—it should be said that what principally moves to this is that very illumination which begins in the innate light and reaches its culmination in the infused light. . . . And this is clear from experience, if anyone would have recourse to the hidden depths of his own mind.[8]

It is quite evident that Bonaventure's understanding of the revelational encompasses every aspect of all that exists. It is equally evident that, far from limiting revelation to the idea content of sacred writings or even accepting the significance of scriptures as the center or norm of revelation, the norm and highest manifestation of the revelational are to be found in the experience of illumination. And this is not to be located in written books, but in the book of life. From this we should be able to conclude that for those who do not know the Gospel and hence cannot obey it there is no loss, since in the life process of experience as they travel *in via* they will receive illumination according to their progressive need and capacity, and ultimately find the completion of revelation in the "face to face" encounter with God in union.

It is not an exaggeration to recognize that Bonaventure has reduced the function of the Scriptures to a pragmatic remedy for a portion of the damage of sin with its impairment of man's vision. And this is only *a* remedy, not at all *the* remedy insofar as he expressly presumes that the non-Christian is fully *in via* and hence actively reading and responding to the book of life. His appeal to "Christians, Jews, Saracens and heretics" is interesting in that he is encompassing all the kinds of peoples with their differing religious Traditions, at least as known in his day. This universalism in revelation is not at all confined to scriptures, and the norm of judgment thus rests within the experience of illumination open to *anyone* who "would have recourse to the hidden depths of his own mind."

In the light of this range of meaning for the revelational we must conclude that at least for some theological schools the revelational is a universally applicable category not limited to a single conceptual content but rather open to the entire range of religious experience. Further, revelational religious experience is not confined to the "extraordinary" or "higher" or "mystic", but is properly—not by accommodation—anything which in any way manifests what the word "God" is intended to identify.

Within this framework there is no distinction or division possible between "revelational" and "non-revelational" traditions. There are simply historically different kinds of revelational traditions—the differences in kind to be accounted for not on the basis of *content* (true/false; fullness-of-time/primitive; complete/partial; and so on), but on the recognition of the variety of authentic historic *situations* in which men experience and share.

III

The non-Western Traditions have been classed as non-revelational and have usually accepted that classification. This must be seriously challenged, not merely because we find theological systematizations from the past which define the revelational broadly enough to include them, but because any thrust toward convergence demands that we discern and develop all unitive dimensions. The narrowness of the conceptualization of revelation generally accepted since the Reformation has resulted in an imperialistic sense of exclusiveness on the part of Christian theology—which has even prevented Christians from taking Judaism and Islam seriously. Political imperialism imposed this narrowness on all non-Western Traditions so effectively that it is still rarely questioned. Without doubt, universalizing the revelational and locating its normativeness in the consciousness of the inner depths of experience of the Sacred, and this as shared, will be very disturbing for all Traditions, East and West, for it will demand the emergence of a true reverence for the authenticity of each Tradition. This reverence will not be satisfied by the politeness of superficial dialogue nor by simplistic indifferentism. Even a passing consideration of this "new" theological dimension seen functioning in heretofore "non-revelational" Traditions can indicate the scope of the impact to be felt.

In any reconstruction of the main lines of the religious experience of the historic Buddha we can see this broader sense of revelation verified.[9] Taking up the account at the moment of the crisis which calls him to seek enlightenment, we find Gotama confronted with the archetypal challenge of destruction experienced in the immediacy of existence. In three symbolic encounters he is brought face to face with old age, sickness and death. Understanding what old age means to life, that it slowly but inexorably destroys mind, beauty and strength, he is appalled that the world goes on day by day unperturbed at the doom awaiting every man. He can no longer imagine enjoying life if he must fear his own aging. He next realizes what sickness is, capable of afflicting anyone at any moment, making a sense of personal security impossible, a constant threat worse than old age, and yet once again the world takes no notice of what this must mean for life. Finally, he is grasped by the reality of death, the end fixed for all, the sentence of total loss for all that lives, and he despairs that none seems aware of what this should mean for the value of life. He can now find no happiness in anything, knowing that all even now is in the process of destruction.

This is a moment of complete disillusionment—not merely in the discovery of the destruction embedded in existence, but even more in the awareness that men are capable of blinding themselves and living in the illusion of security. Westerners often evaluate Buddhism as a commitment to total pessimism, but this is only true in one dimension, in the statement of the *problem* demanding enlightenment. The Buddha's encounter with the negation of existence is not the conclusion of an analytical intellectual procedure but the existential confrontation with the crisis of meaning: at the core of the experience of living there is no security, no substance, no permanence—all is every moment passing away. It is the terrifying discovery of *meaninglessness*. But something immediately happens to him in this moment of disillusion. He recognizes that he is one with other men. Knowing that there is no ultimacy at the core of his own existence as such, he ceases to have pride in his own vitality and strength—we are told that suddenly all hatred and contempt for others were removed from his mind. This is the beginning of the positive transformation *from illusion,* taking place in the very act of disillusionment, the origin of the reversal of what would seem to be the dead-end of meaninglessness.

It is characteristic of much of contemporary Western existentialism to conclude the exploration of the significance of reality with the affirmation of meaninglessness. Man is thus doomed to tragedy. The ultimate evaluation of all existence is negative and pessimistic. The most that can be expected from the noblest that is in man is something akin to the Buddha's concern for others insofar as he recognizes a human fraternity among the doomed. A certain congeniality for Buddhism has grown within some Westerners—or, better, a congeniality for their reading of Buddhism. For they stop woefully short, resting with the Buddha's recognition of meaninglessness and his first personal reaction to it, and fail completely to see the immediate reversal of negative to positive. The Buddha does not conclude his religious quest with the recognition of meaninglessness: this is the beginning point. The confrontation with meaninglessness precipitates his quest: is there a way to destroy meaninglessness, is there a way to achieve liberation? His new vision of himself in relation to others, that no one is superior since all are doomed to old age, sickness and death—to meaninglessness—is not his new life commitment, but the opening phase of the progressive revolution his life must undergo if he is to attain to liberation.

In the narrative of the Buddha's life, Gotama is now confronted with a holy man, one who has perceived man's tragedy and has embarked on the quest for resolution. He tells the future Buddha that he has left all—home, kinsmen, possessions, the taste for life—since none has any significance, and now searches for the end to extinction. And Gotama realizes he too must take up the life of homelessness and become a searcher. At this point we should be aware of the actual interrelation of the negative and positive (and, pessimism and optimism) in Buddhism. The evaluation of existence *as we know it* as negative implies an opposite. If life is substanceless there must be something which is not. Buddhism is pessimistic about the human condition as it is, but is supremely optimistic about what man's destiny *can be*. And hence the calling coming to man in his encounter with meaninglessness: turn away from this illusion—implying that there is "something else": the extinction of extinction.

In legend Gotama embarks upon his quest by taking up the traditional asceticism of the wandering holy man, practicing austerities almost to the point of death in the attempt to achieve enlightenment. In the end he discovers he is as far from his goal as when he began and so concludes that this is not the way to freedom. And so he abandons the ascetical way and resolutely gives himself over to meditation, to penetrate the ultimate meaning of transitoriness and emerge into the illumination of its opposite. We are told he began his meditation intent on the discovery of the ultimate reality of things and the goal of existence. (And we should note again the positive orientation of the quest as a turning away from the false.)

The meditation is recorded as a series of steps. In the first phase, he attains to the conviction (not merely as an abstract intellectual conclusion, but as an encounter) that this world of change as it passes away from moment to moment is totally without any inner substantiality. In the second phase he becomes convinced that there is also nothing substantial in the world of becoming. In the third phase he passes from the awareness of the negatives to the positive foundation of liberation; he sees that it is blindness that keeps man from realizing the falseness of illusion, of thinking the world as it passes away and becomes is substantial, and so illumination destroys ignorance and with the cessation of ignorance there cease old age, sickness and death and all that is false. Perceiving *what is not* is the *liberation from* illusion which in itself allows the *liberation into* enlightenment to take place. Gotama becomes the Buddha, the Enlightened, as at this point of encounter he passes through the experience of liberation from the *false* into the *true*. And so this final phase is spoken of in terms of permanence: having reached the state of all-knowledge, he is in the state of changelessness, Nirvana, all that is opposed to transitoriness.

Once again it is appropriate to recall the expression of this as an act of travel *to the Other Shore*.[10] The actual movement *from* and *to* integrally involves the change in the state of consciousness and of existence. Achieving the Other Shore is experiential, yet can be conceptualized only reflectively in terms of negating what *this* shore of transitoriness and meaninglessness seems to be. The *entire process* is the Wisdom of the Other Shore, the symbol of enlightenment.

It should be self-evident that, in spite of the great differences in orientation between the Christian and the Buddhist experience, what *happened* to the Buddha is properly revelational in character. If we think back to Bonaventure's symbolism we can recognize the *reading* of the two-fold book of life (and antecedently the book of creation as well) in the *experience of liberation* of the historic Buddha and of Buddhists following this way to enlightenment.

If we are inclined to accept Buddhism within the category of revelation we must do so seriously, not in an accommodational manner. The discussion evolved in this chapter does not have for its purpose the adjustment of the revelational to make it a "little broader" or more sensitive to anything like "primitive revelation." The consideration of Buddhism, brief though it is, is designed as a demonstration of the unrealistic narrowness of the Western *conceptualization* of revelation, and hence the demand placed upon theologians to redefine the category to encompass properly the wide range of meaning belonging to the revelational. Of course in this process we must expect major adjustments or revisions within the Western Traditions since revelation could no longer be thought of on an exclusivistic basis, and, even more important, since the *historic* character of the actual revelational process as pluralistic in scope cannot be defined in terms of single chronological sequences or isolated historic moments. Thus, not only must the three sequences of Judaic, Christian and Islamic revelational chronology be related to each other (which they are not at present—"Old Testament," "New Testament" and "Qur'ān" representing self-contained closed histories of revelation), but the recognition of revelation-in-historic-process calls for the acceptance of parallel and overlapping chronological history whose full evaluation depends on the kind of meaning achieved in the coming convergence. Put simply, to close a canon of sacred scriptures at a certain point with a certain content only defines one dimension of the revelational process, a dimension certainly authentic in itself but having a further authenticity in convergence with others.

IV

Are there non-revelational forms of religion? The answer depends on the definition given to the category, and hence the Bonaventurian theology of revelation would clearly insist that all Traditions are revelational (especially recalling Bonaventure's appeal to the agreement of "Christians, Jews, Saracens and also heretics" on the first principle, cited previously). Yet there are Traditions which specifically deny any revelational character to their origin or content; cannot (must not?) these be non-revelational? Again the answer must depend upon the definition of the category. Close examination will readily demonstrate that Traditions denying a revelational character to themselves are rejecting a narrow definition—they have merely acquiesced in the assumptions made by other Traditions as to what constitutes the revelational.

Once again Confucianism can provide us with a very demanding testing of our proposal. In all contacts with Western religion, Confucianists have always maintained that the *Way of Ritual* is not derived from any source but human insight, both in terms of the ways of tradition as shaped in history and in terms of the wisdom of the sages interpreting tradition as mediated by continuing scholarship. As mentioned before, Westerners like Ricci were delighted to find "remnants" of "primitive revelation" in the Confucian Tradition, but certainly agreed with their Neo-Confucian colleagues that Confucianism was a philosophy and standard of ethics and *therefore* not revelational (probably not to be classed as religion, either). This seems to be confirmed by Confucius himself when he declares that he is not one who has innate knowledge but is simply one who both loves the past and studies it.[11] We should recall again the disciple's explicitation of the nature of the Master's teaching:

> Tzu-kung said: We are permitted to hear
> the Master's views on culture
> and the manifestations of the Good *(jen).*

> But he will not speak to us at all
> on the nature of man
> and the Way of Heaven.[12]

Yet as we have already seen in considering Confucius as a "proto-theologian," his vision of the relation of things expressed through *ritual* was such that he surely goes beyond the "merely traditionalist" or "merely ethical" to point all things to the Transcendent while never speaking directly of it. Hence, *to know the meaning* of the Great Sacrifice would be to know all that is under Heaven.[13]

While he denies innate knowledge in himself, Confucius claims that it is Heaven that begat the power *(Te)* which is in him.[14] There is power, *Te,* in everything and everyone, all derived from the Principle hypostasized in traditional language as Heaven, so Confucius is not claiming that he uniquely has received Heaven's power. But he is claiming that Heaven's power in him is unique because it is the power-in-him. It is in himself as empowered that he loves and studies the past, that is, the previous manifestations through ritual *(Li)* of the relation of earth-man-society-cosmos with Heaven. Recollecting the central concerns of primitive Confucianism discussed earlier, we can represent the core of Confucius' Way of Ritual, *Tao Li,* in this systematic structure:

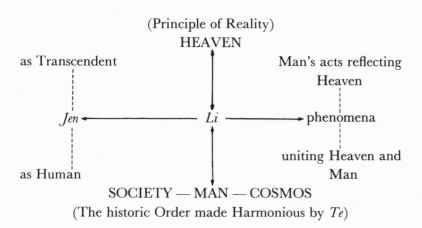

(Principle of Reality)
HEAVEN

as Transcendent   Man's acts reflecting
                                                                  Heaven

Jen ◄─────────── *Li* ───────────► phenomena

                                                        uniting Heaven and
as Human   Man

SOCIETY — MAN — COSMOS
(The historic Order made Harmonious by *Te*)

It does not seem possible to escape the conclusion that Confucianism at its core is properly a religious Tradition and properly revelational in character. In the Bonaventurian concept of the revelational, *Li* is clearly the center of the book of creation and the book of life, made existentially real for man by the implanting in him of the power of Heaven whereby the Principle of Reality is integrally present in what man does.

Confucianism as a Tradition has always dealt with *Li*. Confucius taught about culture (the things of life) and the manifestations of *jen* (the doings of life) as these show forth what the Principle of life is. The *Tao Li*, therefore, is markedly secular in character yet with a reverence for the secular which bears silent but eloquent witness to what the secular actually is in the vision of Confucius: the revelation of Ultimacy.

If in *Li* we can discern the book of creation and the book of life, perhaps we can discern the book of scripture in the writings of the Teacher of *Li*. Apart from the oral teachings preserved in the more ancient portions of the *Analects,* there are several texts ascribed to Confucius himself, among which the most important for us is the *Great Learning.* In it Confucius presents his vision of the Harmony to which man in history is called. Perhaps in this writing we can perceive the difference between innate knowledge and the *seeing* which occurs in one embodying *Te*—the difference between the revelational as an infusion of ideas from without and as a reading of what we encounter on the Way:

THE GREAT LEARNING

What the Great Learning teaches is:
to manifest illustrious virtue,
to renew the people,
and to rest in the highest excellence.
The point where to rest being known,
the object of pursuit is then determined,
and, that being determined,
a calm unperturbedness may be attained.
To that calmness there will succeed tranquil repose.

In that repose there may be careful deliberation,
and that deliberation will be followed by attainment.

Things have their root and their branches.
Affairs have their end and their beginning.
To know what is first and what is last
will lead near to what is taught in the Great Learning.

The ancients who wished to manifest illustrious virtue
throughout the kingdom first ordered well their own states.
Wishing to order well their states,
they first regulated their families.
Wishing to regulate their families,
they first cultivated their persons.
Wishing to cultivate their persons,
they first rectified their hearts.
Wishing to rectify their hearts,
they first sought to be sincere in their thoughts.
Wishing to be sincere in their thoughts,
they first extended to the utmost their knowledge.
Such extension of knowledge
lay in the investigation of things.
Things being investigated,
knowledge became complete.
Their knowledge being complete,
their thoughts were sincere.
Their thoughts being sincere,
their hearts were then rectified.
Their hearts being rectified,
their persons were cultivated.
Their persons being cultivated,
their families were regulated.
Their families being regulated,
their states were rightly governed.
Their states being rightly governed,
the whole kingdom was made tranquil and happy.

From the Son of Heaven to the mass of the people,
all must consider the cultivation of the person
the root of everything.
It cannot be when the root is neglected
that what should spring from it

will be well ordered.
It never has been the case
that what was of great importance
has been slightly cared for,
and also that what was of slight importance
has been greatly cared for.[15]

The vision is certainly secular. It is concerned with man in his world. But it is a *vision* of the secular: the Harmony to be found/manifested in the process of fulfillment. The purpose of the *Great Learning* is to *manifest* virtue, *renew* people, *achieve* completion—how is this *not* revelation in religion?

Obviously, the question of the meaning of the revelational goes far beyond a theological redefinition of systematic categories. In the previous chapter we were content to develop a notion of the theological process as being appropriate to any Tradition, whether revelational or non-revelational. It is evident that the considerations developed here challenge this distinction as irrelevant in any sort of context not simply culture-bound to one Tradition or to one theological interpretation of a Tradition. In the light of being able to extend the range of meaning of the revelational, the development of an empirical form of theology urged previously is even more important. As the range of the revelational includes such a wide variety of truly diverse dimensions (both among the several distinct Traditions, and internally with reference to scriptures, the "secular," "inspiration," and the like), theology as a systematizing discipline must have the capacity to address many types of issues and modes of approach in religious experience.

The most important challenge of all, however, is to the religious experience of those of the Western Traditions. Concentration upon religion as revelation has been within well determined limits, basically within the texts of sacred scriptures. This concentration has been dynamic and creative, and it has been the source of a sense of stability and security. The challenge is thus direct and bold: can they embrace a "revelation explosion" in the convergence of religions? The Christian intellectual tradition

in theology can and does speak of a universal character of the entire revelational process (and we find comparable instances in
Judaic and Islamic theology), but what is the reaction *in religious
experience* when this ceases to be a theological generality and is
present existentially as we confront the sharing of experience?
We must remember that for Bonaventure and others up to this
point, the "Jews, Saracens and heretics" were usually existentially remote from individual and communal involvement. The
book of creation and the book of life could be thought of on so
grand a scale of cosmos and history that actually one could remain psychologically within the covers of the book of scriptures
—the Scriptures as Revelation received and closed within one
text only.

Scriptures as writings witnessing to Revelation evoke a unique
response from the one capable of reading them experientially:
This is a Book like no other book. In a convergence of religious
experience, the challenge is to a new unique response: These are
Books like no other books. It is the rare Christian who can "feel"
the Qur'ān when it is in his hand (and not merely in "reverence
for reverence," but authentically), will he be able to "feel" the
Great Learning?

It never has been the case
that what was of great importance
has been slightly cared for,
and also that what was of slight importance
has been greatly cared for.

CONVERGENCE
AND
COMMITMENT

I

In all of our exploration of a possible new meaning for theology to meet the expected situation of religious convergence, we have attempted to approach the issue in ways generally free from cultural and religious bias. Of course the success of any such attempt must be relative. A genuinely neutral approach is simply not possible. At most we can hope for a level of generalization broad enough in its implications to allow another who is not bound within the same context of culture and religion to perceive potential points of contact, interchange and serious dialogue. The intent of the present undertaking is to contribute to and possibly stimulate the kinds of interrelationship which are beginning to take shape. And thus, far from being a product of the convergence process in terms of an *answer,* our only realistic purpose must be to aid in the creation of a *need.* If we can demonstrate that some sort of coherent and significant means of communication can be developed among the heretofore separate traditions, and if the circumstances of converging civilization force us to

166

take one another seriously, then each tradition—simply to survive—will inevitably discover the need to enter creative relationships with the others.

The generalized theory of theology for religions we have been
trying to develop does seem to escape the narrowness of clear-cut
identifiability with any one tradition. The dialectical relationship proposed for the *theos-* and *logos-*categories, the proposed
definition of theology as drawn from the actually differing experience-expression processes of the principal historical religions,
and the potential of continuity between such a structure and
comparable science theory structures of our contemporary civilization should justify our hopes for a positive opening to one another. At the same time, generalization alone would betray our
fundamental concern. We are not seeking a least-common-de-
nominator religion nor any of the various subversions of mutual
authenticity discussed at length previously. The generalization, if
valid, is made so that we will be able to fashion an instrument of
theological language enabling serious religious conversation to
take place, leading to whatever convergence is to be. Most characteristic of theological discipline as conceived here is the creativity of the theologizing process. Creativity is rooted within actual
individual men as experiencers, and within the communities they
form together as sharers. Therefore, not only is it impossible to
achieve a level of generalization genuinely not reflective of any
cultural or religious bias, it is in no way desirable. Our undertaking would be sterile indeed if we thought we could content ourselves in developing theology for convergence without insisting
on carrying this development forward immediately into theology
(or theologies) *in* convergence.

And so we must make explicit the relationship between theological general structure and creativity, the systematization of
experience-expression and individual/communal commitment-
conviction, and religion and the religious man. A pre-condition
to this is honesty. The theologian does not exist in a vacuum and
hence must identify himself clearly in terms of his actual religious
tradition. His creativity derives from that tradition and he must

recognize this and express it unambiguously. But from the nature of what he is attempting to do he must also recognize that he is moving away resolutely from any negative narrowness of separatism. Already present in his commitment and conviction must be the consciousness of the authenticity of his tradition as not determined by isolation (even though the tradition arose, took shape and was stabilized up to this point in relative isolation). He must now be aware of the essential differences marking the traditions off from one another as the complementing elements of the unity-in-diversity now possible for the first time. A theologian working creatively within the convergence of religions must presuppose that unitive convergence itself, as a principle and as an actual process, is integrally part of his own historic tradition—which he can recognize as a potential within the claim to universality which every historic religion has in some form, and in the assumption embedded in each tradition that it can meet successfully the historic human condition and hence the present condition of convergence.

Even more important is the honesty of acceptance required on the part of those who do not identify themselves with the theologian's tradition. In evaluating his attempt to enter the situation of convergence, they must be candid in making plain whether or not they are committed to convergence from within their own traditions. If this honesty is not present and manifested it seems very unlikely that they could evaluate his attempt as anything other than a new guise for the old imperialism. Even if they conceded his own good intentions, communication—talking *with*— simply could not be taking place. To participate in a dialogue of convergence we all must be aware of the trust called for: at every speaking each must be seeking to move out toward the other, toward an unknown point of meeting, from a clearly recognizable point of departure, from which we do not actually depart! The peculiarity of the convergence process is that we must not think we are leaving or abandoning traditions for someone else's or for a new construction, but we are bringing traditions into contact with the expectation that when they are no longer isolated we will be able to discover how each in its own authenticity has even greater significance in interaction with the others. This has all been said, but within the context of the development of a general theory. We must now be willing to take our exploration into the milieu of an actual tradition.

We are thus testing the authenticity of the individual tradition insofar as it attempts to participate in convergence. For this we are presuming the two dimensions of honesty indicated above. We are also assuming that the historic traditions are being "called into unity" and hence that this is integral to their authenticity. The theological task is to discern this calling in the historic development of the tradition to this point and creatively to project at least something of what a fulfillment of this calling would mean for the tradition in question and the others converging with it.

Although the question of the fact of religious convergence—that it is taking place, or is about to take place—is bound up completely with the convergent development of our civilization, for the Christian there is a special level of concern insofar as he has become involved in the pattern of inter-Christian convergence which has been emerging during this century. We can debate as to whether Christian ecumenism is controlled by factors independent of a more general convergence, or whether ecumenism is the still-immature first-fruits of the new unity, possibly its exemplar, probably uniquely valuable to others as an almost laboratory type of experiment, and so on. One thing is certain: an unexpected pattern has taken shape within Christianity which from this point onwards will influence intimately all that Christianity can come to be in the future. However Christians will finally come to understand their relationship with non-Christian Traditions, even these first few years of ecumenical experiment have resulted in the recognition of the need to repudiate the negative evaluations and seek positive ones. The first thirty years or so of ecumenical development among Christians increasingly pointed in this direction, and during the last ten to fifteen years some preliminary concrete explorations were undertaken. One

thinks immediately of the crisis in Christian-Jewish relations precipitated by the theory and practice of Nazi ideology, certainly
calling for the most serious self-examination on the part of the
Christian not only with regard to at least passive participation in
the Hitlerian holocaust but also an equally serious reassessment
of the implications in the identification of a Judaeo-Christian
heritage. We are also reminded of the pioneering efforts of theologians such as de Lubac[1] with his concern for the potential of a
creative confrontation of Christianity and Hinduism and Buddhism, and Tillich[2] with his realization of the need to recast the
traditional Christian concerns in the light of a positive encounter
with the East and with ideological structures which in some sense
share responsibilities with religion. And we are aware of the dramatic witness borne by Teilhard de Chardin[3] to the positive convergent drive together of the core of Christian Faith and the vision of science and the world it is evolving.

Perhaps most dramatic of all is the recent revolution within
Catholic Christianity, moving so unexpectedly into the full current of ecumenism and, however awkwardly, bringing to the fore
explicitly for the first time within any contemporary Christian
body the acknowledgment of the need to establish positive and
significant relationships with non-Christian peoples and heritages. Though tentative, faltering and woefully short, a first step
in what could be a reconstruction (or new construction) of religious relationships with Judaism became a major issue of the Second Vatican Council. Also from that Council came the decision
to establish formal ecclesiastical channels of communication with
non-Christian religions and with the parareligious ideologies,
paralleling the organizational structure fostering inter-Christian
ecumenism. Again, our concern is not with the practical effec-
tiveness of any such steps but with the fact that steps of this sort
have been undertaken at all and are accepted as appropriate to
the proper internal development of Christianity on the part of
most of the Christian churches.

II

In the rather short history of ecumenism, first inter-Christian and now at least vaguely also Christian/non-Christian, primary emphasis inevitably has been placed upon religious pluralism. We have been pursuing the many levels of pluralism—social, legal, ecclesiastical—to dispel ignorance of facts, to gain insight and respect for religious traditions not our own, to solve practical and ethical problems raised in law and society by the pluralistic condition, and to combine efforts in areas of common concern and agreement. In general a remarkable state of mutual good will has replaced most of the hostile entrenchments of the past, in retrospect no mean accomplishment indeed!

Yet the new-found religious euphoria must not be mistaken for the goal of ecumenism, as, unfortunately, it certainly does tempt those who prize ecumenism as peaceful coexistence to do. *Theological* ecumenism as the quest for universal unity entailing a oneness of commitment has not only received secondary emphasis, it is usually discretely deemphasized. The real issue of religious commitment is avoided. We have been learning to respect the fact of the individual's commitment, but we have not been studying what commitment is—for the individual, his tradition, the total human community and the developing history of convergence. All too rarely does anyone undertake an exploration of commitment as such. If those who seek to contribute to the development of convergence would do so effectively, they must move from the level of generality to the demanding task of understanding specific religious commitment. As a necessary pre-condition to such study, we must have learned to respect the individual in his commitment, but this itself is not even the beginning of the true problem.

Everyone is involved in a religious commitment of one type or another: he is committed to one tradition, and hence excludes others; he is committed to a highly individualistic approach to religion, and hence is relatively indifferent to the specific traditions as such; he is indifferent to religion; he is opposed to religion. These divisions, with their possible subdivisions, represent in each instance an involvement in religious commitment. No one is uncommitted. Not to choose is to choose. No one is without an approach to Reality. No one is valueless. The implication of such a recognition is that commitment arises from *involvement* and not from conviction: conscious conviction depends upon the real experience of involvement for which the mind seeks adequate expression. We are committed to a particular religious tradition or system insofar as we are consciously convinced that it is the *expression* of the actual relationship to Ultimacy, however we think we have touched it in living. The religious system is the medium of our consciousness of involvement in that relationship.

Buber's analysis of the significance of the apparent atheist points up this dimension sharply. Believing himself godless, he gives himself over entirely to addressing the *Thou* of his own life experience as a *Thou* which cannot tolerate limitation by another; the Ultimacy touched within his address to his own selfhood is *an* experiencing of what men call God.[4] A similar insistence on the intimacy of the experiencing of Ultimacy within the constitution of the self is implied directly in Aquinas' identification of the nature of God with Existence:

As long as a thing exists, therefore, so long must God be present to it according to its manner of existence. But existence is innermost in each thing and most fundamentally present within all things. . . . Hence it must be that God is in all things, and innermostly.[5]

The individual is not committed to his convictions, but to the involving Reality conceptualized in his convictions. Convictions must be respected in that they are the conscious expression of the integrity of the conscious person. But the basis for convictions must be opened for exploration, from within and without, since no man can presume an absoluteness for his own consciousness. Religious commitment as experiential, therefore, must be viewed as dynamic, not static. The quest for truth demands the constant attempt to conform our conceptualizations to reality. However much we succeed, we realize nonetheless a degree of failure: we are simply unable to reduce the Ultimacy touched by our experience to a concept.

The recognition that everyone is committed—*involved* and with *consciousness*—demands the correlated recognition that the investigator must proceed from within the context of his own commitment-conviction. Thus, a Christian's approach to religious convergence must be Christian or it will be false—as false as the presumption that one can proceed without convictions, neutrally. Similarly, the Judaist must work from the consciousness of his commitment, the Muslim from his, and so on.

We must face a methodological paradox: to understand and contribute to the process of convergence, we must work from the orientation of our divergent commitment-convictions as they are now, and not pretend that we stand at some future point of unity looking backward upon divisions of the past. In effect, we presume that convergence to a common point is taking place, the general direction from each beginning-point can be plotted to some degree, but we must move toward the unitive center from the present diversity of origins. As stated often before, we do not know how the convergence will actually take place, how so many and so different traditions can ultimately become one. Each knows only his own starting-point and the direction toward the others that convergence is taking him. The methodological task, therefore, is to begin moving toward others from within our own committed tradition: discover lines of possible unification within each conscious commitment, seek to extend these and be responsive to the constant demand for renewal and reformation which must follow.

Working from within the context of actual personal commitment to Christianity, our task is to attempt to formulate a theological structure which can embrace positively the historic condition of pluralism of religions, the movement toward convergence and the Christian assertion of unique and universal authenticity. The mere statement of such an assertion, of course, seems to erect a massive barrier against any movement other than conversion. Yet it is quite clear that from the beginning as an integral factor in the core of Christianity universality has been asserted, and it does not seem possible to refrain from the assertion if what moves into convergence is to be actual Christianity. The theological structure we seek, therefore, must succeed in formulating the assertion without imperialistic implications.

The maintenance of the integrity of the Christian commitment is not to be construed as a denial of the integrity of any other religious Tradition. The Christian *as such* cannot presume to speak for the other Traditions. He attempts to work toward others from his proper context, hoping he will meet others working toward him. To be true to himself and to be able to contribute realistically to eventual religious unity the Christian first of all must interpret the process of convergence for his Christian Tradition. He must develop an understanding of unity in the context of the Christian religious experience if a Christian is to be able to experience unity.

III

Although religious pluralism is such an obvious and often painful fact in many contemporary societies (especially if we extend this plural relationship to include ideology), most approaches to its analysis are limited to a consideration of pluralism as a *de facto* condition of society and to the practical problems to which it gives rise. Thus, taking the plural condition of American society as an exemplar, we are concerned with socio-political patterns which allow for the survival and freedom of separate traditions, or with problems of church-state relations, religious-secular education and the like. Theologically, we are concerned with freedom of conscience, religious exercise and witness. An especially difficult area of problems is the extension of the framework of religious pluralism to embrace religious-secular pluralism. Not only does this entail two apparently antagonistic world-views, but it also involves forms of religion far removed from the principal traditions, raising additional problems for religious convergence on any level. (Thus, traditional religious forms have difficulty in evaluating what is often called liberal religion; and so, in the setting of most Christian forms, in what sense is non-theistic Unitarianism "Christian," apart from its historic origins?)

However broad the coverage of issues and problems, we rarely attempt to face the basic question suggested by a pluralistic society. We accept the *fact* of pluralism, but do we evaluate the *function* of pluralism in the on-going formation of human community?

For most, pluralism is a necessary evil arising quite simply from ignorance or from the inability of large numbers of men to agree to a single pattern of thought and expression covering areas of experience extending further than the directly tangible. It would appear that societies are pluralistic only because no practical means can be found to eliminate differences. This type of approach is not without objective foundation. We do find religious traditions, or at least elements in them, involved in ignorance, and in seeking to dispel the ignorance we can eliminate the tradition. Tolerance of religious belief rarely means total indifference to a concern for "truth" or "objectivity." Even the most tolerant are opposed to human sacrifice, though clear-cut examples of this type are rare in contemporary societies.

In the history of American religion there have been (and still are) major conflicts involving one or another religious group (the religious form usually being at an extreme of the range of types). We think of the long struggle of Mormonism over the issue of plural marriage, with the resultant major change in the concept of the millennial Zion. The individual and group health problems raised by Christian Science have resulted in various actions by the civil courts with consequent shifts of emphasis within the tradition. The current struggle of the Amish against involvement in welfare programs and civil standards of primary and secondary education is the struggle to maintain the independence of socio-cultural forms necessary for the survival of the religion. In each instance the larger society tends to view the particular issue as ignorance (or worse!), and thus implicitly intends to introduce radical changes in the traditions to "solve" the problem, while explicitly simply dispelling the point of ignorance.

With regard to the inability of men to agree on religious conviction as the basis of *de facto* pluralism, this was certainly a prime factor in the formulation of the American Constitutional position of non-establishment of state religions and the protection of individual conscience. Long before the extension of this federal position to the states by the Fourteenth Amendment, states with established churches, such as Massachusetts, disestablished them because they had become politically unviable in the face of growing local religious diversity. As with the problem of ignorance, the political impossibility of effecting some externally objective basis for judging between religious systems does explain much of the rise of *de facto* pluralism. But it does not lead us to any evaluation of pluralism itself.

A positive alternate to these essentially negative approaches views religious pluralism as a benefit and even as a necessity for a free political society. In this instance pluralism functions in part as a guarantee against the domination of society at large by any single religious or ideological body. Although this is certainly an effect of pluralism this approach is not religious (or ideological) in orientation. Rather, it presumes an inevitable antagonism between socio-political values and religious values, it gives preference to socio-political values, and it is ultimately unconcerned with any attempt to realize the thrust of religion toward unity. It is a positive approach in that it seeks to foster the continuance of pluralism, but not for the sake of the objective religious values.

In all of our previous considerations of the emergence of religious convergence we have been building an approach to pluralism in terms of the more general human condition of individual consciousness, social communication, the evolution of traditions and the continuing progress and refinement of knowledge. We recognize that the variety in religious systems is not the result of blind chance and blunder and of insurmountable ignorance, but is the legacy of sincere, insightful and often heroic men seeking truth for themselves and for all mankind. Hence a positive understanding of religious pluralism must reflect the process of human existence itself.

Pluralism can be expressive of two totally opposed aspects of interhuman relationships. Pluralism can be negative, expressing and effecting division between individuals and groups. Negative pluralism excludes, opposes and disrupts intercommunication. Such pluralism reflects the presence of two or more mutually incompatible issues or complexes of issues, each calling for the rejection and repudiation of all competitors—at least according to the active interpretation of values being made by the participants. In terms of concrete examples, one thinks almost immediately of the partition of the Indian subcontinent expressing the divisive Muslim-Hinduist negative pluralism (in spite of the lavish tradition of unitive pluralism of forms within Hinduism).

Any negative pluralism presumes that one position at most can be valid and every other position is *totally* invalid—except, perhaps, in what are evidently non-essentials. In actual societies this divisive condition at best allows for an uneasy coexistence—usually quite uneasy since each knows he must be always on the defensive if he is to survive, for even the benevolent indifference of his neighbor can inadvertently generate destructive forces and conditions (as witness the Amish, caught up, with the best of intentions, by the juggernaut bureaucracy of the Social Security program[6]). With our usual emphasis on the problems of pluralism rather than on pluralism itself, we tend to take pluralism in this negative sense.

But if we inquire why divisive pluralism should arise at all, we come upon an enlightening paradox: religious diversity arises from a common attempt to discover, understand and communicate what can be experienced and known of Reality. The diversity occurs because of the uniqueness of each individual seeker, his community and the condition of their moment of history. But the diversity is profoundly meaningful because of the ultimately singular character of the object of the quest. Men do not seek different "Reals," and their differences, therefore, cannot be evaluated against each other, some being "realer" than others. We are confronted, then, with pluralism as positive, expressing and effecting unity between individuals and groups: the Real in a diversity of experiences and expressions.

The religious pluralism of any actual society is a concrete though limited exemplar of what is implied in general religious convergence. The scope is not as great and the tensions not as radical. But a positive pluralism exhibits the complementing dimensions of unity in terms of the Ultimacy toward which the many individuals tend and in terms of the unification of the many into a oneness which is not a uniformity. The pursuit of positive pluralism demands a condition which is virtually always present, namely, the sincere intention of the religious man to seek the truth, to embrace it when discovered, and to reject relatively unrealistic ways of understanding or communicating it in favor of more appropriate ways. The rejection of negative pluralism entails the attempt to discover and discard the actually divisive elements—meaning elements which divide men from a genuine realization of truth sought, and hence which divide men from one another.

This process is not achieved simply by abandoning the *de facto* historic divisions, but by eliminating the bases of the divisiveness heretofore characterizing such divisions, and so transforming divisions into complementing bodies of a greater organism. The ultimate thrust of pluralism is not any type of reduction but a liberation of true individuality free to interpenetrate and generate new life. Any realization of positive pluralism is absolutely opposed to a simplistic indifferentism or relativism of personal commitment-conviction: one way of religion is just *not* the same as the others, and if they are to be brought together it must be through the authentic action of the fully identified participant who has experienced and continues to experience within his tradition.

IV

In the historic situation of the drive toward ecumenical unity which characterizes the Christian community today, a theoretical structure based on the distinction between positive and negative pluralism might be received readily enough, but it must meet the challenge of two questions. First, can it be a practical structure as well as theoretical? And second, can the Christian commitment to Christ and Church as uniquely authentic be maintained and communicated?

The claim to authenticity is immediately bound up with the claim to universality, in which Christianity sees itself as revealed for the ultimate fulfillment of all mankind. Christians have continually faced the need of giving conscious meaning to this vision of universality within specific historic contexts. In the setting of earliest Judaic Christianity, Christians naturally enough conceived of universality in terms of Jewish hopes for the restoration of the earthly kingdom. The ejection from the synagogue and the eventual destruction of Jerusalem and dispersal of the Jewish Christians necessitated a shift of context for universalism, although the types of Israel, Jerusalem and Zion maintained their mystic hold through the reading of the Scriptures and the imagery of the liturgy.

The Pauline de-Judaizing of Christianity with the vigorous growth of the Greek and Roman churches outside the synagogue gave rise to a new understanding of universality in terms of the Classical world, its tradition and the Empire. The new continuity of Christianity with this world resulted in the integration of the ancient philosophers and their ideals, culminating in the work of such men as Augustine. External structure was effected also with the adaptation of the geographical-political concept of the civil diocese; as the Empire encompassed "all" the lands with this interlocking hierarchy of provinces, so the Church came to express universality juridically as well as ideologically.

The fall of the Empire and the Christianizing of the invaders gave rise to Christendom as the universalist structure with its centuries-long struggle against the world of Islam. Continuing the geographic diocese of Roman Law, Christendom was also structured in the feudal interrelation of persons and loyalties theoretically applicable to every human being. The cultural revolutions of the age of discovery transformed this Christendom-universality into a religious imperialism, calling for the direct overthrow and annihilation of non-Christian Traditions. In our own time the reassertion of the integrity of the peoples and cultures of Africa and Asia has swept away Christian religious colonialism, and so we seek a new vision of the universality implied in our commitment to Christian authenticity.

With the exception of the initial incorporation of the Graeco-Roman Tradition within Christian consciousness of its significance for all mankind, no stage in the historic growth of Christianity beyond its beginnings within Judaism has been formed with a positive attitude toward the actual condition of the majority of men. Individuals have been accounted for in terms of Christ: the dying-and-rising of Christ with its transformation of life somehow involves every individual, past, present and to come, whether one is aware of it or not. But if left at that, while speaking of the non-Christian, such an approach leads to peculiar conclusions: everyone is indeed fulfilled by Christ, but not necessarily by Christianity, that is, by a pattern of life centered upon an awareness of relationship in Christ. The consciousness of the fact of Christ for all men never reaches beyond a small numerical minority. Hence, one's religious way of life seems to be a matter of practical indifference, and most men are not involved in what is traditionally referred to as the "economy of salvation," but in an economy of ignorance. Clearly the general theological tendency has been to *explain away* non-Christianity rather than face it as a real part of the actual world in which Christianity has its supposedly unique and ultimately fulfilling significance.

Is Christianity actually the way of life for all men? Or must the Christian presume that the way for most men (as seen by the committed Christian) quite literally is the *way of ignorance?* If such a suggestion is abhorrent to the Christian and non-Christian alike, then a positive approach to universality must be developed meeting the actual condition of the human race, the realities of the historic religious Traditions and the witness the Christian must bear to his experience of Christ for men.

Perhaps we can find the foundation for a positive understanding of authenticity-universality in the theological relationship of Christianity to Judaism, a relationship actually based on pluralism. It is important to note that this Christian-Judaic pluralism has been limited (except for the very first years) to a theological relationship, and this has been very narrowly conceived on both sides. Christians have generally been concerned only with Judaism (or, more properly, selected aspects of Judaism) up to the time of Christ, denying validity to the continuing Judaic Tradition. And the continuity of Judaism to the present certainly embarrasses Christians since on such a narrow evaluation it should have disappeared long ago.[7] Judaists on their part have consistently negated any significance for themselves of Christianity, regarding it at best as a sort of non-respectable heresy attacking the integrity of the Jewish community which has given rise to a sectarian gnostic gentile religion, often the source of vicious anti-Semitism. Thus, up to this point Christian-Judaic pluralism has been limited to a restricted theological pluralism, not a pluralism of Traditions, and this condition must constitute the basic challenge in any serious Christian-Judaic convergence.

From the beginning Christians have seen an organic unity of the Way of the Covenant with the Way of Christ. The Covenant experience and tradition prepared for Christ, whereby a people was drawn on historically to be able to receive the sought-for fulfillment. Christ fulfilled the Covenant in the experience of the first Christians, the *Jewish* Christians. Granted that Christ's significance extends beyond the historic Israel (and hence that Israel itself must have a broader meaning than the ethnic community), yet for Christian theology the irreducible relationship is *Christ fulfilling Israel's quest.* The most profound expression of this relationship is the compelling theme *in the fullness of time:* the moment of maturity, the completion of preparation, the quest achieved. It would be meaningless to attempt to conceive of the historic occurrence of Christ apart from such a moment. *Fullness of time,* thus, is two-fold: the seekers and the sought.

Yet all men are seekers and, as Christians must affirm, not in vain. The Christian is conscious of Christ as their fulfillment whenever they live, however they seek. *Fullness of time,* therefore, must be a *fullness of times.* The many religious ways of life that have come from man are not meaningless in the face of Christianity. Without them there could be no *fullness of time* in Christ for each people, either in the life of the individual or in the life of the community.

If Christ and Church are inseparable, the Church somehow must be involved in Christ's *fulfillment of all mankind.* If Christ comes to man in the fullness of times, so does the Church. If Christ is actually universal, so is the Church as the community of Christ-experience. Christianity, the process of Christ-life, is thus bound up with every way of life. This universal significance is positive for both Christian and non-Christian. The Christian can perceive a meaningful continuity between whole ways of life and his own, rather than an atomizing of the human race and a repudiation of human religious response. The non-Christian can no longer be the object of religious imperialism or paternalism, for the Christian must approach him truly as a brother serving his need to maintain continuity with the past and the still unfolding present and its future.

Christianity would now be understood as actually embracing the entire human race, past, present and future—all *somehow* involved with the reality of Christ. Those conscious now of Christ accordingly are called to a ministry of service to *brothers,* not to conquest. The Church, then, is a priesthood, consciously bearing Christ to the world.

This type of approach to universality involves the Christian in neither syncretism nor indifferentism. Christianity does not seek to absorb other ways of life but to fulfill, insofar as Christians in concert with their brothers find the ways to openness so that a sharing of experience can take place. Christianity must not be twisted into a competition for man's allegiance—whether men realize it or not Christians must recognize their religious experience-expressions as integrally Christian. It is not that any path man chooses leads equally to God, but that every path is in some real sense the Christian path in that the many are also always the one, that having arisen and taken form in isolation from one another nonetheless all mean something more now together. The Christian task is to extend the awareness of Christ, not as if Christ is coming into the world as an alien, but the Christ in whom all things already exist. The fullness of time in Christ for each religious community as a sacred tradition comes insofar as Christians succeed in awakening men to the actuality of the Presence of Christ. There is no reason to expect the dangers of syncretism or indifferentism as Christians realize their unity with all mankind. For Christians this universal unity is unavoidable: Christ and Church are one, dwelling one in the other, and Christ is come for all men. Historic distinctions, functions and structures within religious Traditions are real. But participation in an ultimate unity is also real if Christianity is actually of universal significance.

If we look back to the earliest period of the Church, we find in the de-Judaizing dispute at least a partial exemplar for an authentic Christian approach to unitive pluralism. We tend to forget that Christianity not only first appears within Judaism, it is native to it. The community at Jerusalem together with all the apostolic leaders saw Christianity and Judaism as inseparable. In the dispute raised by Paul on behalf of the newer gentile communities, advocating the discontinuance of the observance of the prescriptions of the Torah, it was the Jewish Church of Jerusalem which gave the decision. Later Christians have usually thought of the conclusion as the Pauline Churches allowing the Jewish Church to maintain its customs; obviously the exact opposite was true: the Jewish Church allowed the gentile Churches to be gentile!

But there are two even more important meanings to this event. First, until the issue was raised by Paul, Jewish Christians evidently never adverted to any distinction between what only later could be seen as "Judaism" and (or, better, versus) "Christianity." There was no discernible polarization or tendency of one to pull away from the other. The tensions recorded in the Book of the Acts[8] are taking place within or among synagogues. And second, because of this undivision, the Jewish Christian experienced in himself and in his total community a complete sharing of religious experience at once fully the Tradition of Judaism and fully the forming Tradition of Christianity. This was a unique moment in the history of *both* Traditions, and an absolute demonstration of the validity of the unitive experience. If the Jewish Christian communities had not been destroyed in the general destruction of Jewish Palestine by the Romans there is no reason to think that a truly Judaeo-Christianity would not have continued to exist. Although it cannot be an example of *convergence,* this initial integral unity of Judaism and Christianity must be taken seriously if we attempt to explore the implications of unitive convergence. There is a terrible tragedy in the thorough, mutual rejection of each other which has hung like a curse upon both Christians and Judaists for twenty centuries. Forgetting the openness of the Apostle James and his Jerusalem community when they allowed the gentiles their own observances, Western Christians even went so far eventually as to decree the death penalty for any Jewish Christian who in any manner dared to observe the Tradition of the Torah!

The positive insight into essential values which was achieved by the settlement of the Pauline controversy is of the greatest importance in attempting a formulation of unitive theology. The notion of *conformity* as the criterion of *authenticity* was rejected. Authenticity is to be determined by the realism of the response as one *objectively showing forth Christ* as He occurs in actual history. Difference in response need not indicate conflict in objective meaning. Rather, insofar as we must recognize the dynamic character of history as a process we must also recognize the inevitability of many differing moments of response corresponding to the dynamics of a fully historic Christ.

All too often we should assume from the structures employed

by Christian theologians that the Christian experience is not only rooted in historic events but is confined to certain past events. However it is to be explained or communicated conceptually, the Christian experience of Christ is in the present: Christ alive *now*, participated in *now*. The fullness of time we have been speaking of, then, is not one *completed* in the past, but one which *begins* at a certain moment now past. And so if we expand this to a fullness of times, we insist even more that Christ as man is continually coming and thus that a fulfillment in the fullness of time cannot be a termination of a preparation but must be the on-going and open-ended life of the Tradition(s). Or, to put it in another traditional framework, the incarnation did not take place, it is taking place—*being* man must mean *becoming* man, and if so then in the way man becomes: individually/socially, experiencing/sharing, in each single historic moment and in the continuum of the entire process of history.

It seems the Christian must come full circle if he is committed to a Christianity authentically universal. If men's relationship to God takes place historically through this actual man Jesus Christ in whom man-and-God and manhood-and-Godhood are fully united, then this actual man Jesus Christ must be genuinely historical, and relating to God through Him must take place in a genuinely historical manner—He must always be becoming in on-going history and we must always be seeking to relate through Him as *we* are. Unity in Christ is processual and not terminal, and thus fulfillment in Christ does not terminate but thrusts forward—and not just as an indeterminate seeking, but as embodied in the sacred traditions.

V

Each of the world religions is unique and universal: unique in that at the core of each is a distinct central experience of man-and-Ultimacy not to be found duplicated elsewhere, and universal in that this core experience is of supreme significance for all men. It is the ability of a tradition of religious experience to *speak* to *other* men that calls us to recognize it as a *world religion*. And since such *speaking* takes place at different times according to the changing situation of men, the very identification of those that are the *great traditions* is a part of the open-endedness of the historic process. A tradition which seems closed in upon itself today with nothing to say beyond the narrow limits of its own community tomorrow may be the revealing voice of the Sacred calling forth a further creativity from man. Each no longer isolate tradition is an integral dimension of all the others, and a man cannot participate in one without in some real way participating in all in the totality now emerging in them together.

We have spoken of a fullness of times for Christianity, but if this is not to be the pattern of annihilation-and-succession, then there must be a mutual fullness of times for all the dimensions-traditions. Such fulfilling moments will, of course, be as different in content and impact as are the traditions, but they will be authentic moments in the historic process of religion if all participants take each other seriously.

That word crops up again and again, and its intent is clear. With even the best will possible, there will always be the temptation to undercut the participation of "others" in convergence. The Christian, with a proper sense of the reality of Christ, will be tempted to feel that Christ-consciousness actually in convergence with the substance of other Traditions would inevitably overwhelm them, reducing them at best to providentially prepared introductions to Christianity. If we suggest that this is not the significance of Christ-consciousness in convergence, then it will sound as if we were subverting the reality of Christ.

There is no way to argue through to an understanding of the impact of convergence, true convergence. It must be felt. If it is, then this *experience* will lead us to the realistic *understanding* of convergence. At any point prior to the moment of impact we can only know the limits of the meaning of convergence—significant unity of the different Traditions which remain authentically themselves. Perhaps the worried Christian should be challenged on another level. What does he really believe of Christ and the authenticity of Christianity—in the language of current biblical theology, how can he presume that the existential discovery of *all* of the mighty acts of God will destroy the act of God in Christ?

And comparable challenges must be placed before the participants of all the Traditions. When Christ is taken seriously will that annihilate all the worlds of men who have been dwelling in the Sacred all these centuries, or will it enable them to begin to make one world out of many?

These questions can only be answered through experience, and to be willing to experience demands much of us, especially as this unfolding experience is new. We fear the insecurity implicit in a new experience and this betrays our innermost temptation to infidelity: we want the experience of the Sacred to make us feel secure—we do not want the consciousness that the mighty acts of God must be our acts, our creativity, our responsibility.

The ambiguity of our situation in religious convergence was expressed centuries ago at the very beginnings of Christianity in the words of Christ. We have carefully avoided any attempt to resolve this ambiguity, but now we must.

He who is not with me is against me, and he who does not gather with me scatters. (Mt. 12:30)

Yet:

Anyone who is not against us is for us. (Mk. 9:40)

Because:

Anyone who does the will of my Father in heaven, he is my brother and sister and mother. (Mt. 12:50)

APPENDIX
MODELS
AND THE FUTURE
OF THEOLOGY*

EWERT H. COUSINS

In the environment of his new civilization, modern man is open to a variety of experiences that have not been available before. To his bewilderment and enrichment, space and time are being compressed; different types of human experience throughout the world are converging; and new possibilities are opening on the horizon.[1] To encompass the fullness of his new experience, modern man must enlarge his consciousness. The secular theology that drew traditional religious man into the modern world must now expand to encompass the richness of religious experience. For the man of the future must be in command of his full psychic potential. He must be scientific and technological, mystical and mythopoeic, intensely individual and autonomous and at the same time deeply related to all men and the cosmos. He must be a man of the past and of the future so that he can live the present in all its complexity. The era of specialization of experience has passed. Those levels of the psyche that modern man had

* Published originally in *Continuum*, vol. 7, no. 1, Winter-Spring 1969, pp. 78–91.

previously stifled to develop science, industrialization and technology must be opened once again. He can no longer be fractional man, with only a portion of his powers activated. It is only with the full resources of his psychic life that modern man can move into the future.

Modern man is not limited to the experiences of a single historical epoch, and he is not limited to the experiences of a single culture. This convergence of cultures will have an enormous effect on man's religious experience, for he will have to learn to live in a complex religious environment. That modern man has already begun to open to the varieties of religious experience is indicated by the development of the ecumenical movement. In the meeting of world religions, the missionary of the future will not be attempting conversion, in the classical sense, but convergence. What form this convergence will take is difficult to predict because we are not fully in the environment that will provide its matrix. But this much seems to be clear: the man of the future will have to find new ways to enlarge his religious experience in order to be responsive to the religious experience of others, not merely to the simple varieties within his own tradition, but to the radically different religious experiences of those from other great traditions.

What is the role of the theologian at this time? He can help modern man move into his future. As one learned in his own religious tradition, the theologian can bring its resources and wisdom to self-consciousness. As one sensitive to the religious experience of different traditions, he can discover ways of relating positively across cultural barriers. As one responsive to the times, he can join with others in a common openness to the future. In the recent past the theologian's task was marked off by the forms of secular culture that had emerged in Western civilization. Since religious belief had become divorced from developments in secular culture, the theologian submitted his beliefs to radical criticism and demythologizing in order to bring them in line with the limits of secular experience so that religion would be meaningful to modern man. But the very technology that led to the need for demythologizing has produced an environment in which multi-levelled experience is possible. Instead of engaging in demythologizing and radical criticism, the theologian will be called upon to bring to light the richness of his tradition. Having long been alienated from the mystical, cosmic and mythic levels of consciousness, modern man must now open himself to their depth and power and integrate their resources into his full conscious life. It is in this process of rediscovery, reintegration and expansion that the theologian can make a special contribution.

The theologian must know the forms of religious experience of his own tradition, and he must know the concepts and symbols in which they are expressed. He must have a method that will bring these forms into self-consciousness with precision and clarity, that will be rooted in the historical process and that will be open to the experiences of other religious traditions. At the present time there is an idea operative in several fields that can prove especially helpful to the theologian. It is the idea of model, which has been gaining increasing attention in mathematics and the natural and social sciences.[2]

Aware of the complexity of their subject matter, the natural sciences use various models to express the various aspects of the material world. For example, light manifests aspects of a wave and of particles. The data is so complex that the scientist must use two models—that of a wave and that of particles—for understanding the phenomenon of light. The fact that these models are opposite and irreducible one to the other does not deter the scientist because he can employ them as complementary models. The social sciences and psychology have adopted the concept of model and have used it in studying human behavior. For example, the social scientist may use the computer as a model, seeing man as a data-processing mechanism and studying his social interactions as information input, processing and feed-back. At times the model may be used in a picturing or suggestive manner; or it may be elevated to a more theoretical and mathematical level, where it will provide a conceptual and mathematical matrix to give form and coherence to a variety of data.[3]

The widespread use of the model method at the present time is not a matter of chance, but rather grows out of our historical situation. For the model method opens man to the complexity of the world. It is based on the assumption that reality is multi-dimensional and that there is a need for a variety of forms to reflect it. Since there is no need to use a single model for his vision of the world, the scientist can be open to the historical process and development. He does not have to freeze new developments with static forms. If another model will throw light on reality, he will use it. And in this on-going process, he always holds his models open to testing; they are hypotheses that must be verified and criticized in a number of ways. Thus the method has openness and flexibility but at the same time allows great precision and clarity. This set of qualities recommends the method for theology at the present time.

There have been attempts recently to apply the model method to theology.[4] Inspired by the use of models in science, the theologian looks upon theological language and symbols as models that reveal something about God just as scientific models reveal something about the physical universe. According to Ian Ramsey, for example, both theology and science are concerned in their own way with the disclosure of a mystery.[5] Because of the vastness, complexity and depth of the physical universe and the limits of human mind, it is appropriate for the scientist to use models. In that way he can obtain some knowledge, but only part of the whole. The same can be said for theological concepts and symbols. Theology is concerned with the ultimate level of religious mystery, which is even less accessible than the mystery of the physical universe. Hence our religious language and symbols should be looked upon as models because, even more than the concepts of science, they only approximate the object they are reflecting. As Ramsey has said:

. . . The number of models is legion—strong tower, king, father, shepherd . . . waves, particles, elastic strings. . . . Many are

logically disparate at that; nor is there any finite bound either to
verification and empirical fit. It is in these ways and for these
reasons that we may say that theorizing by models is the understanding of a mystery whose depths are never sounded by man's
plumb-lines, however long and however diverse these lines may
be, however far developed. It is in these ways that both science
and theology provide us with different and characteristically
different understandings of a mysterious universe.[6]

To use the concept of model in theology, then, breaks the illusion that we are actually encompassing the infinite within our
finite structures of language. It prevents concepts and symbols
from becoming idols and opens theology to variety and development just as the model method has done for science. Yet there is
a danger that it will not go far enough, for it may not take
sufficiently into account the level of religious experience. The
theologian may copy the sciences too closely. He may take the
scientific method as a normative model, or he may so shape his
use of the method that he emphasizes those aspects of theological
models that most correspond to scientific models. In so doing, the
theologian may not take into account the subjective element at
the core of religion. Science seeks knowledge of the physical universe. Although subjective factors enter into this knowledge,
subjectivity does not play the central role that it does in the area
of religion. The religious experience has a depth that has no correlate in our experience of the physical universe. The religious
experience touches the innermost part of the person. It may be
felt as coming from outside: as revelation, grace or divine illumination; or it may appear as the discovery of the hidden depths of
one's soul, the finding of the true self or the touching of the
ground of the soul. It has a creative power that expands one's vision and opens new ways of seeing the world. It may be experienced through symbols or language, or it may not. Although it is
most subjective and personal, it is not without its own structures
or forms, which can be studied in a variety of ways.

To be comprehensive, then, a theological method must take
religious experience seriously and deal adequately with its varie-

ties both in the past and in the future. As a step in this direction, we propose extending the model method into the area of religious experience. This would involve building a two-level approach to the model method. One level would deal with religious experience and search out what we will term "experiential models." By this we mean the structures or forms of religious experience, the term "experiential" implying the subjective element and the term "model" implying the varieties of religious experience. The second level of the method would deal with the expression of religious experience in words, concepts and symbols: for example, Biblical imagery, Christian creeds and theological systems.[7] This is the level of what we will term "expressive models," the term "expressive" suggesting the formulation of the experience and the term "model" the varieties of expression. These two levels—experiential models and expressive models—would form the basic structure of a method to be employed extensively over the history of theology with an orientation toward the future.

To extend the model method into the realm of religious experience has the value of opening the theologian to the varieties of religious experience—or in our terms, the varieties of experiential models. This variety stems from two sources: the vastness and incomprehensibility of the Sacred, from which the experience emanates; and the complexity of man and of the human situation in which the revelation is made. For example, Rudolf Otto has described the numinous as having opposite qualities, for it is both *tremendum* and *fascinans*.[8] Thus the manifestation of the Sacred as *tremendum* would produce a different experiential model from that resulting from its manifestation as *fascinans*. On the other hand, the variety may come from man. For example, he may experience redemption as liberation from personal sin and guilt; or he may experience it as the restoration of the image of God within him. These would be different experiential models. Further, he may experience the presence of God in places set apart as holy, such as churches or shrines; or he may experience the presence of God throughout nature. In all of these cases we would be dealing with different experiential models.

A great deal of research has been done in the area we refer to as that of experiential models. The theologians can draw from the pioneering work of William James, *The Varieties of Religious Experience*,[9] the basic analysis of the numinous by Rudolf Otto in *The Idea of the Holy*,[10] the studies in primitive religion by Mircea Eliade,[11] the studies in religious psychology by C. G. Jung,[12] and the recent empirical studies in the phenomenology of states of consciousness by Masters and Houston.[13] This material has not been sufficiently integrated into theology. Since theologians have been concerned with the symbols and concepts in which traditional religious belief has been expressed, they have not always faced squarely the forms and structures of religious experience itself. This is partially due to the fact that there has been need of a comprehensive theoretical framework for dealing with the experiential level in a systematic way. The model method seems well suited to this purpose, and the distinction between experiential and expressive models may offer at least a tentative structure for developing such a theoretical framework.

It is important to know the experiential model that stands behind a particular expressive model. This is made difficult by the complexity of expressive models and the fact that much religious language is drawn from non-religious areas of experience. Man has expressed his religious experience in words, concepts and symbols derived from the social and economic structures in particular cultures. For example, Christians have spoken of their liberation from evil as a redemption, a buying back. One way to determine what this language means is to study its origin in history, through etymology and cultural linguistics, in order to see what area of social custom it is reflecting. This task is not made easier as theology progresses, for these expressive models often become more complex. For example, in medieval theology Anselm developed an elaborate theory of the redemption based on the concept of satisfaction. Not only did he use intricate rational argumentation, but drew from feudal customs and perhaps from Roman and Germanic legal practices.[14] In studying Anselm's satisfaction theory, the theologian would have to explore the legal and sociological models at work in his thought. But this would not be enough. The theologian would not reach the heart of the matter until he uncovered the religious experiential model behind the expressive models. He would have to be on his guard to avoid a type of reductionism, in which symbols are simply reduced to cultural models.

In Anselm's case the very legal model acts as an expressive model for a much deeper religious experiential model. Rudolf Otto has pointed out that Anselm had a consciousness of the mystery of sin on the level of depth religious experience.[15] In the history of religion, the mystery of evil has been reflected in a variety of experiential models. The specific experiential model in Anselm's case was the overpowering burden of guilt. At its center is a grasp of the infinite dimension of evil which causes the burden of guilt to weigh down on man with such force that he is unable to remove it and needs the Infinite itself to lift the burden.[16] It is this depth religious experience that Anselm conveys by sketching the outlines of the feudal lord to whom satisfaction is due because of his offended honor. This image and Anselm's exploration of the infinite dimension of evil and the inexorable logic of guilt coalesce to form an elaborate expressive model. Once the underlying experiential model has been isolated and explored, the theologian can chart the correlations between the experience and its expressive model. It is here that various theories of language and prediction can be brought to bear: for example, Aristotelian analogy, Platonic participation, Otto's theory of schematization or Ramsey's concept of disclosure models.[17]

One of the constant dangers in theology is to remain on the level of expressive models and to fail to take into account experiential models. In the case of Anselm's highly complex expressive model—and of Western medieval theology in general—this would lead to a science of verbalizations and conceptualizations. A theology that would neglect the entire experiential level and concentrate solely on expressive models would lack vitality and depth. It would be lifeless and abstract. This was the danger with the catechetical method and the scholasticism of the theological manuals. Throughout the history of theology, there has been a constant return to experiential models. When the expressive models become too elaborate or disengaged from experience or convey the wrong level of experience, theology has attempted to return to its roots, as it did at the Reformation and in the thinking that led up to and surrounded Vatican II. The return to experiential models is usually brought about by a return to the early Christian experience especially as witnessed by Scripture.

Not only do expressive models reflect and express religious experience, but they shape it as well. This is especially true of cosmological models. Since primitive times, man's cosmological models have been bound up with his religious experience and belief. In Western civilization from the time of the Copernican revolution and the rise of modern science, cosmological models have been at the storm center of religious controversy.[18] Since they are so basic, a shift in cosmological models can radically affect the entire structure of one's belief. The change from the Ptolemaic to the Copernican universe affected man's self-image and challenged some of his cherished religious ideas. From the time of the Renaissance and into the Nineteenth Century, debate raged over the status of the cosmology of Genesis in relation to that of science. With the aid of Biblical scholarship, theologians began to see cosmological models as expressive models in which man formulated his religious experience. Thus the theologians could accept an evolution in cosmological models which did not undermine the ultimate significance of the Genesis narrative. For they could see in the Genesis cosmology the expressive model of a religious experience that transcends the primitive cosmology.

Not only do expressive models evolve, but experiential models evolve as well. At the present time we are entering a change on the experiential level that is as radical as the Copernican revolution was on the level of expressive models. Man is ending his isolation on the earth and moving into outer space. For the first time man is actually experiencing the Copernican universe and not merely understanding it intellectually with the aid of an abstract model of the solar system. The more that the earth-bound community shares in space travel, the more their experience of space will take on new dimensions. Because of the close tie between cosmological models and religious models, this new experience of space will open new varieties of religious experience and give new meaning to cosmological symbols. If man's experience of the desert sun shaped the model of the Sky-God and if his experience of the fertile land shaped the model of the Earth-Mother goddess, then his new experiences in outer space should shape new religious models and add new dimensions to his old models.[19] The classical religious symbols of up and down—programed into the human body by the force of gravity—will lose their experiential references in a state of weightlessness. Light and darkness, sky and earth, sun and stars, distance and speed will be experienced differently in outer space. As man views the earth from outer space, he may grasp more profoundly the meaning of his traditional earth symbolism. And his new elemental experiences of the vastness of space may awaken in him experiences akin to the experiences that stand behind primitive man's cosmological models. The man of the future, then, as earth-dweller and space-traveller, will learn to live in a complex cosmology: with multiple experiences of space and an enlarged spatial symbolism. The theologian, having learned from the theological debates of the past over changing cosmology, can be sensitive to the expressive nature of cosmological models and so help modern man open to the religious significance of his new experiences in space.

Closely associated with cosmological models is the experiential model of the cosmic sense. This is the experience of being related to the entire cosmos, whether the cosmos is looked upon as the physical universe, the historical process or the entire human community. This sense of being related to the whole has long been submerged in Western culture, since the rise of individualism at the time of the Renaissance. Yet many signs indicate that it is emerging again, having been evoked by science, space travel, the communications network around the earth and a rising sense of solidarity felt throughout the world. The cosmic sense is emerging, not as a romantic escape to nature or a loss of individuality in the collectivity, but on a deeper level and as the matrix of the experience of the future. This has great significance for the theologian. From primitive times the cosmic sense has been bound up with man's religious experience. It played an important role in the Bible and in the theology of the Greek Fathers and of the medieval West. The doctrines of Christology, redemption and the sacraments, for example, have not only an individual level, but a cosmic level as well. Since it is often this cosmic level that is expressed in religious symbols and concepts, many of the traditional expressive models can be understood only when situated within the experience of the cosmic sense. In the light of the re-emerging cosmic sense, then, the theologian can better understand a major level of his past tradition; and with this historical awareness, he can be more sensitive to the religious dimension of the cosmic sense in our time.

The emergence of cosmic Christology in our times challenges the theologian to re-examine the Christological models of his tradition. The Christian experience of Christ has generated a variety of models. Throughout the history of Western theology, there has been an increasing emphasis on the historical Christ and redemption from evil as contrasted with the cosmic Christ and the completion of the universe. In the Middle Ages devotion to the humanity of Christ intensified the West's concern for the concrete and the particular. Hence it was the historical Christ in the concrete circumstances of his earthly life who became the moral model for the individual Christian.[20] Satisfaction theories of the redemption, such as Anselm's, gave expression to the West's sense of the burden of guilt. At the time of the Reformation, these trends became thematic in the Christology of redemption in which Christ, through his death on the cross, has brought personal salvation to the individual Christian and liberation from the burden of sin.[21] Elements of this classical Western model can be seen in such a contemporary movement as existential theology.[22] If the cosmic sense is emerging as a widespread cultural experience, then the theologian will have the task of examining both the individual and cosmic models of Christology and of charting their interrelation. This is especially needed if the theologian is to approach the future with the fullness of his tradition's resources.

The very process carrying modern man into his future is drawing the religions of the world toward an encounter that is unique in human history. At the present time the theologian has a twofold task: to make available the richness of his own tradition and to become aware of those elements in his tradition that will make him sensitive to the heritage of other world religions. He will have to penetrate beneath the layers of expressive models to contact the underlying religious experience. He may find little similarity between the religions of the East and West in the area of language, concept, economic, sociological and cosmological models; for they have developed largely independently of each other and in diverse cultural settings. Yet by going to the level of experience, he may be able to establish points of contact across cultural lines.

Through a variety of examples we have attempted to illustrate differing aspects of a theological adaptation of the model method. Of course, the instances have been proposed as illustrations and not as definitive positions. It has been impossible to amass all the evidence on a particular point, and in some cases much research has yet to be done. Some examples are open to different or more complex interpretations. For our purposes they can serve as working hypotheses to be tested by various means of verifications. In this form, they can indicate the general lines of an approach which we can summarize as follows: (1) Distinguish between expressive and experiential models. (2) Begin with an expressive model at a given point in history and explore all levels of language, concept and symbol and all the cosmological, social, legal, economic forces in culture that have entered into the formation of the expressive model. (3) Bring to light the experiential model that the expressive model is formulating; this presupposes an awareness of the varieties of religious experience and some attempt to view these varieties in a systematic fashion. (4) Explore the multiple relations between expressive models and experiential models: in past history, in relation to contemporary culture and in reference to the future, not only in one's own tradition but in the context of world religions.

Such a method can aid the theologian in his task of assisting modern man to move into his future. Inspired by the model method in the sciences, it can open theology to the varieties of experience that are emerging on the horizon of an expanding and converging world. At the same time that it opens theology to variety, it calls for an extensive use of analytic precision and critical evaluation. Within this context, the theologian can face squarely the complex issue of norms in theology. He can examine the question of the absolute claims of an historical revelation, the uniqueness and normative nature of religious experience, pluralism of religious forms in the face of the claims of historical revelation and individual religious experience. He can view these normative issues in the complex context in which they are emerging in modern times. Such a method would hopefully teach modern man not to trap himself in his models; he can break out of the limits of his own cultural forms and open himself to the richness and complexity that the future holds for multidimensional man.

NOTES

CHAPTER I: NOTES

1. Cf. Margaret Mead's structural analysis of the emerging socio-cultural dynamics, under the categories post-figurative, co-figurative and pre-figurative, in *Culture and Commitment* (Garden City: Natural History Press: 1970).
2. This early formula is carried forward by Augustine and Aquinas to authenticate theology built upon Greek philosophical systems.
3. J. P. Migne, *Patrologiae cursus completus: series Graeca*, XI, 1574 (Paris: J. P. Migne: 1857–66).
4. J. P. Migne, *Patrologiae cursus completus: series Latina*, XXII, 871.
5. J. P. Migne, *P.G.*, LV, 156.
6. Martin Gerbert: *Scriptores Ecclesiastici de Musica*, I, 3 (1784).
7. While evaluating the general stance of Christian theology toward the other Traditions negatively, nonetheless we must acknowledge the historical base of a contemporary theological concern with convergence. Under the influence of Hegel and Schleiermacher, some Nineteenth Century German Protestants began to conceive of the absolute character of Christianity as the culmination of a universal divine religion to be found imperfectly formed but actually present in other religio-cultural traditions; the historic Christ was the heightening of the divine-human spirit, not its only effective presence. Whatever its limitations, such a view was a significant move away from the earlier exclusivism that apart from the Christian Church there simply was no religion of divine origin. This approach became operative among Catholic theologians only in the Twentieth Century, and especially through the work of Rahner had its creative impact on the formulations of the Second Vatican Council. Some Twentieth Century Protestant theologians began to move away from the earlier culmination view, rejecting the notion of the other Traditions as merely preliminary to Christianity or as imperfect primitive expressions; various new approaches were attempted, generally relativistic in character with a deemphasis or disestablishment of Christocentric uniqueness. Whatever the criticisms that must be made of

them (in the line of relativism rather than relativity, or scientistic reductionism, or the like), they have done much to open new dimensions of
theological speculation and expectation. This recognition stands behind
much of the discussion of convergence in later chapters of this present exploration.

8. W. A. Visser't Hooft: *No Other Name*, p. 116 (Philadelphia: The Westminster Press: 1963).
9. *Ibid.*, pp. 117–18.
10. Will Herberg, *Protestant-Catholic-Jew*, p. 97 (Garden City: Doubleday and
Company: 1955).
11. Visser't Hooft, *op. cit.*, p. 119.
12. *Ibid.*
13. *Ibid.*, p. 121.
14. Karl Rahner, *The Christian of the Future*, p. 79 (New York: Herder and Herder: 1967).
15. *Ibid.*, p. 80.
16. *Ibid.*, p. 82.
17. *Ibid.*, pp. 82–83.
18. *Ibid.*, pp. 84–85.
19. This is not intended to imply a division between "religious" and "secular"
of a sort as to make these two categories alien to each other; insofar as a
proper *distinction* between religious and secular can be made, however, dialogue or action among religions to be *distinctly* religious must center upon religious concerns.

CHAPTER II: NOTES

1. Pierre Teilhard de Chardin, *The Phenomenon of Man*, pp. 251–53 (New York:
Harper and Row: 1965).
2. K. M. Panikkar, *Asia and Western Dominance*, pp. 326, 331 (New York: John
Day Company: 1953).
3. Hendrik Kraemer, *World Cultures and World Religions*, p. 14 (Philadelphia:
The Westminster Press: 1960).

CHAPTER III: NOTES

1. Diego de Landa, *Relación de las cosas de Yucatán.*
2. Bernardino de Sahagún, *Historia General de las cosas de Nueva España.*
3. Juan de Torquemada, *Los veinte i un libros rituales y Monarquia Indiana.*
4. Edward Burnett Tylor, *Primitive Culture* (New York: H. Holt and Co.:
1874).
5. F. Max Müller, *Sacred Books of the East* (Oxford: Clarendon Press: 1879–
1910).
6. Cf., e.g., E. Durkheim, *The Elementary Forms of the Religious Life;* S. F. Nadel,

The Foundations of Social Anthropology; A. R. Radcliffe-Brown, *Structure and Function in Primitive Society.* Beginning especially with Durkheim, many theorists of society and culture have emphasized the functional importance of religion as a center of self-identity for the group or community, and at times have even defined religion as that function.

7. Problems in the alliances of the Nazi ideology/state during World War II illustrate this in contemporary societies; with judgment of racial superiority and inferiority dependent upon identification with the Arian stock of Caucasians, the Nazi regime was inevitably embarrassed by the necessity of an alliance with the Japanese, a situation solved by making the Japanese "honorary Arians" (amusingly, the reverse procedure was not followed; the Japanese Government with their doctrine of the divine race and nation did not declare the Nazis "honorarily divine"). For aspects of the religious character of Nazi ideology, cf. John S. Conway, *The Nazi Persecution of the Churches 1933–1945* (New York: Basic Books: 1968).

8. Justin Martyr, *Apologia* I: 46.

9. Clement of Alexandria, *Stromata* V: 5, 29; 4–6.

10. The interpretation of the conflict between Rome and Carthage almost always presumes that the defeat of Rome would have been a disaster for both civilization and the future spread of Christianity. From Roman roads to Roman law virtually every aspect of the Imperial system is taken as an essential for the foundation of Christianity. Few advert to the fact that if Carthage had won, the Carthaginians would have fallen heir to the Greek Mediterranean civilization just as did the Romans—and the archaeological evidence from the ruins of Carthage indicate a Greek-Punic synthesis already well advanced before the Punic Wars. Christian historians most especially have presumed a special Providence guarding the Latin language, for the Western Christian, at least, the only language fitted for proper theological development; some have gone so far as to identify Jerome's Latin translation of the Scriptures as the inspired *textus receptus,* and until recently Roman Catholic theology always drew exclusively from this version, as commanded by the teaching authority of the Church. No one ever seemed to advert to the fact that the Carthaginians spoke a language closely akin to Hebrew, and so if Carthage had won, the Christian Scriptures would have been written in a language guaranteeing linguistic and cultural continuity with the Hebrew Scriptures.

11. Mateo Ricci, *History.* In retrospect, Ricci's accommodational approach to the establishing of Christianity in China on a Chinese basis appears quite pragmatic. Accepting elements he thought of as vestiges of primitive revelation, he allowed for the overall Confucian philosophy and ethics insofar as these were reminiscent of the Graeco-Roman heritage of the West. But it is difficult to see that he intended anything more than to use what was adaptable in Neo-Confucianism as a wedge to guarantee the acceptance of a thoroughly Western Christianity, which in the last analysis merely spoke Chinese. He certainly did not look forward to a Christian-Confucian synthesis of any sort or to any distinct creativity arising specifically from the Chinese character of Christianity in China. Among fellow Christians the source of opposition to his methods (apart from ecclesiastical politics) centered around fears that non-Latinized Chinese Christians would be *corrupted* by continuing *superstition* and *idolatry.*

12. John Damascene, *Barlaam and Josaphat.* The authorship is disputed, but if not by John Damascene himself, then certainly by one of his school.
13. James Frazer, *The Golden Bough* (original edition, 1890; *The New Golden Bough,* Theodore H. Gaster, ed., Garden City: Doubleday & Co., Inc.: 1959).
14. Cf., e.g., B. Malinowski, *Magic, Science and Religion* (Garden City: Doubleday & Co. Inc.); P. Radin, *Primitive Religion* (New York: Dover Publications, Inc.: 1957).

CHAPTER IV: NOTES

1. Cf. Chapter VII.
2. Jean Jacques Rousseau, *Discourse on the Origin and Foundation of Inequality among Men* (*Collection Complète des Oeuvres de J. J. Rousseau,* vol. 6; Geneva: Volland: 1790–91).
3. As translated in Whitson, *Mysticism and Ecumenism,* p. 168 (New York: Sheed and Ward: 1966).
4. The Way, or *Tao,* as Ultimacy is not conceived of in the Confucian Tradition as *an entity,* such as implied in the Western Rationalists' *Supreme Being.* The theological appropriateness of a non-entitive Ultimacy is considered elsewhere (pp. 102ff and 110ff.).

CHAPTER V: NOTES

1. *Ut supra.*
2. *Mysticism and Ecumenism,* p. 168.
3. Again it must be stressed that *Tao* and "Principle of Reality" do not of themselves indicate a transcendent *entity* as Ultimacy for Confucius.
4. Also it should be noted not all agree that there are implications of transcendence in the passage being discussed; some later Confucianists presume that Confucius' inability to understand the meaning of The Great Sacrifice is due to its technical complexity and antiquity, and hence he finds it impossible to establish all the traditions concerning it. The validity of the interpretation followed here rests upon the continuity of this passage with others of the primitive period of Confucianism which clearly carry transcendent value.
5. *Mysticism and Ecumenism,* p. 176.
6. *Ibid.,* p. 173.
7. *Ibid.,* pp. 174–75.
8. R. E. Hume, *The Thirteen Principal Upanishads; Brihad-Aranyaka* 2. 1–20, pp. 92–95 (London: Oxford University Press: 1934).
9. *Ibid.,* 3.7. 1–23, pp. 115–17.
10. *Ut supra, Chandogya Upanishad* 6.8.6, p. 246.
11. *Mysticism and Ecumenism,* p. 141.
12. *Ibid.,* p. 146.

13. Nikhilananda, *The Bhagavad-Gita,* p. 207 (New York: Ramakrishna-Vivekananda Center: 1944).
14. Hajime Nakumura, "The Indian and Buddhist Concept of Law," in Edward J. Jurji, ed., *Religious Pluralism and World Community* (Leiden: E. J. Brill: 1969).
15. G. P. Malalasekera, *The Buddha and His Teachings* (The Lanka Bauddha Mandalaya: 1957).
16. This reference to *the gods* should make clear, by implication, the important difference between the Western monotheistic designation *God* and the Indian (Hinduist and Buddhist) mythic-polytheistic *gods,* the latter not being conceived of as The Absolute, The Transcendent, or the like, but as superhuman phenomenal entities; similarly, the Indian designation *Heaven* represents another phenomenal mode of existence or another world of timespace in complement to this phenomenal cosmos, whereas *Heaven* for the West is a symbol for the state of transcendent non-phenomenal existence; both these clarifications are important for our evaluation of the meaning of *Nirvana* and/or *Parinirvana.*
17. G. P. Malalasekera, *op. cit.,* pp. 18–19.
18. *Ibid.,* pp. 37–38.
19. *Ibid.,* pp. 48–49.
20. *Ibid.,* pp. 52–53.
21. *Mysticism and Ecumenism,* pp. 158–59.
22. *Ibid.,* p. 134.
23. "Come into" as a phrase represents a difficulty of considerable importance for contemporary Christian theology. Inevitably it carries the connotation of "intrusion" into history from "outside." Whether this is understood according to the classic natural/supernatural structure of scholastic theology or in a modern biblically derived structure of "God's mighty acts in history," any indication of "intrusion" poses a problem for a theological vision of an unlimited and self-contained historic *process of existence.* For our purposes here, "come into" as a phrase is a convenience since it represents a common mode of expression; the intention is to assert a real presence of Divinity in the actual historic process. Hopefully the connotation of "intrusion" can be ignored.
24. Migne, *P.G.,* p. 714e.
25. *Ibid.,* p. 721.
26. *Ibid.,* xlv.
27. *Summa Theologiae,* Part I, Q. 12, A. 2.
28. *Ibid.,* Part I, Q. 3, A. 4.
29. *Liber de Causis,* VI. The Latin terms make the meaning emphatic: God is not an *ens,* an entity or thing or object of any kind (including "the Supreme Being," i.e., "The Supreme Entity"); but God is *esse,* literally: God is "to exist."
30. *Summa Theologiae* Part I, Q. 19, A. 1. The significance of the differing terms, then, should be simply the emphasis being drawn from one or another context of theological interest. But certainly among the followers of Aquinas this is not usually the case; in fact rarely do we find advertence to the logic of the four terms having one meaning. For example, the Sixteenth Century "Grace Controversy" in Reformation Catholicism depended upon the validity of the contrast: God predestined creatures to glory or damnation *either*

because of the Divine Intellect *knowing* what they would do to merit their destiny *or* because of the Divine Will *determining* what capacity they could have to merit their destiny—a meaningless contrast if Divine Intellect *is* Divine Will *is* Divine Existence. For Thomas himself, the only basis for differentiation is according to our mode of understanding and signification —not according to the divine nature itself; cf. Part I, Q. 19, A. 2 ad 1.

31. *Institutes of the Christian Religion,* Book I, I:1.
32. *Ibid.*

CHAPTER VI: NOTES

1. Cf. *Mysticism and Ecumenism,* appendix ii, "Consciousness and the Mystical Process—Psycho-chemistry and the Religious Consciousness."
2. Niels Bohr, *Atomic Theory and the Description of Nature,* p. 1. (New York: Cambridge University Press: 1961).
3. *Ibid.,* p. 12.
4. *Ibid.,* p. 15.
5. Horace Bushnell, *Select Works,* vol. II, pp. 49–50 (*God in Christ*) (New York: Scribner, Armstrong & Co.: 1877).
6. *Ibid.,* p. 55.
7. *Ibid.,* p. 69.
8. *Ibid.,* p. 71.
9. *Ibid.,* p. 74.
10. *Ibid.,* p. 81.
11. *Summa Theologiae,* Part I, Q. 16, A. 1.
12. *Ibid.,* Part I, Q. 16, A. 8.
13. Fazlur Rahman, *Islam,* pp. 31–32 (New York: Holt, Rinehart and Winston: 1966).
14. *Ut supra.*

CHAPTER VII: NOTES

1. Aristotle, *Metaphysics,* VI, i, 1026a19.
2. Cf. Cicero, *De Divinatione.*
3. The technical term "philosophical theology" is a recent one, in use since the last century to connote a special emphasis of philosophy in theology; as used here, philosophical theology expresses a more general notion of the conscious use of philosophical methods and structures instrumentally in early theological systematizing.
4. Clement of Alexandria, *Stromata,* V, 9.
5. Augustine, *City of God,* VIII, 1.
6. Cf. Chapter III, citations from Justin Martyr and Clement of Alexandria.
7. On the same Aristotelian issue, Aquinas later came to the opposite position; cf. *Summa Theologiae,* Part I, Q. 46, A. 1.

8. M. M. Sharif, ed., *A History of Muslim Philosophy*, pp. 221–22 (Wiesbaden: Otto Harrassowitz: 1963).
9. Presuming for the moment that it is sufficient to correlate the final laying down of the experiential materials of each of the Western Traditions with the completion of their canonical Scriptures, the theologizing process begins for Judaism about two centuries later, for Christianity and Islam within a century.

CHAPTER VIII: NOTES

1. In this instance, as so often before, limitation of consideration of the Western Traditions to Judaism, Christianity and Islam is in part a convenience, a limitation to the three historically most important representatives, without any implication that much of what is discussed would not apply to Zoroastrianism and other Traditions not of the Far East.
2. Bonaventure, *Itinerarium Mentis in Deum* [*S. Bonaventurae Opera Omnia*, Vol. V (Quaracchi, 1882–1902)].
3. Bonaventure, *Breviloquium*, II, c. 11, n. 2 (*Opera Omnia*, V).
4. Bonaventure, *Quaestiones Disputatae de Mysterio Trinitatis*, q. 1, a. 2, concl. (*Opera Omnia*, V).
5. Cf. 1 Cor. 13:12—"We see now in a mirror in an obscure manner."
6. The joining of the eye's blindness and the deafness of the interior ear does not constitute a confusion of the *book* symbol; the *book* is not only to be read with the eye, but also to be read out and hence heard, in the context of the monastic *lectio divina*.
7. Bonaventure, *Quaestiones Disputatae, ut supra.*
8. *Ibid. Liber vitae* in this passage refers to the Logos as expression of the Father. In certain other texts in Bonaventure the term *liber vitae* has the more restricted meaning (reflecting its Scriptural origin in the Apocalypse) of the Logos as the basis of the predestination of the just (e.g., *Breviloquium* I, c. 8, n. 2). We use the term *book of life* to refer to human life experience as revelatory. Although Bonaventure does not use the term as such in this precise sense, the usage accords with his system and expresses, in his own genre of symbol, the essence of his vision. For additional material in Bonaventure on the book symbol, cf. Winthir Rauch, O.F.M., article "Liber," in Jacques-Guy Bougerol, O.F.M., ed., *Lexique Saint Bonaventure* (Paris: Éditions Franciscaines: 1969).
9. We are here following the biographical tradition according to the *Buddhacarita* of Ashvaghosha, as condensed by Edward Conze in *Buddhist Scriptures;* these materials as portraying the key elements in Gotama's religious experience can be considered apart from any particular interpretation brought to them by the various schools of Buddhism.
10. Cf. above, pp. 92–93.
11. *Analects*, VII, 19.
12. *Analects*, V, 12; as in *Mysticism and Ecumenism*, p. 168; cf. above, p. 71.
13. *Analects*, III, 11; as in *Mysticism and Ecumenism*, p. 168.
14. *Analects*, VII, 22.
15. *The Great Learning*, as in *Mysticism and Ecumenism*, pp. 165–67.

CHAPTER IX: NOTES

1. Cf. especially Henri de Lubac, *Aspects of Buddhism* (New York: Sheed and Ward: 1954).
2. Cf. especially Paul Tillich, *Christianity and the Encounter with World Religions* (New York: Columbia University Press: 1963).
3. Cf. especially Pierre Teilhard de Chardin, *The Phenomenon of Man; The Divine Milieu.*
4. Martin Buber, *I and Thou,* p. 76 (Edinburgh: T. & T. Clark: 1937).
5. Thomas Aquinas, *Summa Theologiae,* Part I, Q. 8, A. 1.
6. Some Amish groups hold beliefs in Divine Providence which make participation in insurance programs a violation of religious conscience; recent changes in federal Social Security regulations regarding compulsory enrollment of farmers brought the issue to the fore, with government agents ignoring the question of constitutional rights of freedom of religious exercise and collecting the required payments by seizure of property (especially farm tools and animals necessary for Amish self-support!).
7. Not only is this part of the underpinnings of anti-Semitism, but also the basis for some rather crude theological notions, such as the presumption that continuing Judaism exists to bear a salutary witness to faithlessness, or, until the conversion of the Jews the Christian is secure against the cataclysmic Last Day. In a word, Christians have not taken Judaism seriously.
8. *The Book of the Acts of the Apostles,* chapters 6, 7, 15, *passim.*

APPENDIX: FOOTNOTES

1. Cf. P. Teilhard de Chardin, S.J., *The Phenomenon of Man* (New York, 1965); *The Future of Man* (New York, 1964).
2. B. Kazemier and D. Vuysje, ed., *The Concept and the Role of the Model in Mathematics and Natural and Social Sciences* (Dordrecht, 1961); R. Braithwaite, "Models in the Empirical Sciences," in E. Nagel *et al.,* ed., *Proceedings of the Congress of the International Union for the Logic, Methodology and Philosophy of Science* (Stanford, 1960); M. Black, *Models and Metaphors* (Ithaca, 1962); M. Hesse, *Models and Analogies in Science* (Notre Dame, 1966).
3. For a presentation of the various types of models used in the sciences, see L. Apostel, "Towards the Formal Study of Models in the Non-Formal Sciences," in Kazemier and Vuysje, ed., *op. cit.,* pp. 1–37.
4. Cf. especially I. Ramsey, *Religious Language* (London, 1957); *Freedom and Immortality* (London, 1960); *On Being Sure in Religion* (London, 1963); *Models and Mystery* (London, 1964); *Religion and Science* (London, 1964); *Christian Discourse* (London, 1965). Cf. also J. McIntyre, *The Shape of Christology* (London, 1966); F. Ferré, "Mapping the Logic of Models in Science and Theology," *The Christian Scholar,* XLVI (1963), 9–39; W. Austin, "Models, Mys-

tery, and Paradox in Ian Ramsey," *Journal for the Scientific Study of Religion,* VII (1968), 41–55.

5. Ramsey, *Models and Mystery,* pp. 1–21.

6. *Ibid.,* p. 20.

7. Theological systems have other functions besides the expression of religious experience, such as, establishing the validity of belief, defending a position against objections, establishing the coherence and reasonability of the structures of belief. Yet even these functions presuppose a level where the systems are giving expression to religious experience.

8. R. Otto, *The Idea of the Holy* (New York, 1958), pp. 12–40.

9. W. James, *The Varieties of Religious Experience* (New York, 1963).

10. Otto, *op. cit.*

11. M. Eliade, *Patterns in Comparative Religion* (New York, 1958); *The Sacred and the Profane* (New York, 1959); *The Myth of the Eternal Return* (New York, 1954).

12. C. Jung, *The Collected Works of C. G. Jung* (New York, 1953–   ).

13. R. Masters and J. Houston, *The Varieties of Psychedelic Experience* (New York, 1966).

14. Much work has been done as a basis for studying Anselm with the model method: see, for example, A. Harnack, *History of Dogma,* Vol. VI (Boston, 1899), 56–83; J. Rivière, *The Doctrine of the Atonement,* Vol. II (St. Louis, 1909); G. Aulén, *Christus Victor* (New York, 1954); J. McIntyre, *St. Anselm and His Critics* (Edinburgh, 1954); G. Williams, *Anselm: Communion and Atonement* (St. Louis, 1960). For a listing of further pertinent research, see Williams, *op. cit.,* pp. 5–9.

15. Otto, *op. cit.,* p. 53, n. 1.

16. *Ibid.,* pp. 50–59; P. Tillich, *Systematic Theology,* Vol. II (Chicago, 1957), 172–73; C. Anstey, "St. Anselm De-mythologized," *Theology,* LXIV (1961), 18. For a study of redemption from the standpoint of the experiential models of depth psychology, see P. Pruyser, "Anxiety, Guilt, and Shame in the Atonement," *Theology Today,* XXI (1964), 15–33.

17. Aristotle, *Metaphysics,* 1016–1017, 1048, 1070; for a study of Aristotelian analogy in the context of scientific models, see Hesse, *op. cit.,* pp. 130–56. Plato, *Republic,* VI, 506–511; Otto, *op. cit.,* pp. 45–49, 140–42; Ramsey, *Models and Mystery,* pp. 9–10.

18. Cf. W. Stace, *Religion and the Modern Mind* (Philadelphia, 1952), for an analysis of the effect of changing cosmological models on modern religious attitudes.

19. On the Sky-God and Earth-Mother, see Eliade, *Patterns in Comparative Religion,* pp. 38–153, 239–64.

20. The devotion to the humanity of Christ, cultivated by Bernard of Clairvaux and the early Franciscans, can be traced in such writings as Bonaventure's *Lignum Vitae* and the *Spiritual Exercises* of Ignatius of Loyola. Both of these include lengthy meditations on the virtues displayed by Christ in his earthly life, presented as models to be imitated by the Christian.

21. Cf. Aulén, *op. cit.,* but in conjunction with the criticisms of McIntyre, *St. Anselm and His Critics,* pp. 197–200.

22. Such elements are found in the existential emphasis on individuality, authenticity, anxiety and guilt; cf. J. Macquarrie, *An Existentialist Theology* (London, 1955).